East River

• Boluo

Huizhou

SHENZHEN MUNICIPALITY (SHENZHEN SHI)

SHENZHEN
SPECIAL ECONOMIC ZONE

Sham Chun (Shenzhen)

Mirs Bay

Deep Bay

New Territories

Kowloon

Hong Kong

antau Island

0 2 4 6 8 10 Kilometres

0 2 4 6 Miles

Hong Kong and the Pearl River Estuary

South China Village Culture

Series Editors, China Titles:
NIGEL CAMERON, SYLVIA FRASER-LU

South China Village Culture

Culture

JAMES HAYES

OXFORD
UNIVERSITY PRESS

278315

OXFORD   JUN 1 0 2003
UNIVERSITY PRESS

Oxford University Press is a department of the University of Oxford.
It furthers the University's objective of excellence in research, scholarship,
and education by publishing worldwide in

Oxford   New York

Athens Auckland Bangkok Bogotá Buenos Aires Cape Town
Chennai Dar es Salaam Delhi Florence Hong Kong Istanbul Karachi
Kolkata Kuala Lumpur Madrid Melbourne Mexico City Mumbai Nairobi
Paris São Paulo Shanghai Singapore Taipei Tokyo Toronto Warsaw

with associated companies in Berlin Ibadan

Oxford is a registered trade mark of Oxford University Press

Published in the United States
by Oxford University Press Inc., New York

© Oxford University Press 2001

First published 2001
This impression (lowest digit)
1 3 5 7 9 10 8 6 4 2

British Library Cataloguing in Publication Data
available

Library of Congress Cataloging-in-Publication Data
available

ISBN 0-19-591989-0

Printed in Hong Kong
Published by Oxford University Press (China) Ltd
18th Floor, Warwick House East, Taikoo Place, 979 King's Road, Quarry Bay
Hong Kong

Contents

Acknowledgements

A BOOK OF this kind, small in size but wide in compass, leaves one in the debt of a great many people.

Elderly people in the villages of Hong Kong, mostly long since passed away, provided information and insights available from no other source. My sense of the strong Confucian base of traditional rural society at the 'ordinary' level is derived from them. I am deeply grateful to them all, and to my friends among the local leaders who introduced me to them and accompanied me into their homes.

Special assistance has always been provided by Messrs Wan On (溫安) of Pui O, South Lantau, and Yeung Pak-shing (楊百勝) of Yau Kam Tau, Tsuen Wan, who together with Dr Anthony K. K. Siu (蕭國建) and Dr Patrick Hase have long constituted my 'close support team'. Other friends who helped with photographs and information include Ken Haas, Tim Ko Tim-keung (高添強), Dr Betsy Johnson, Dr Solomon Bard, Dr Dan Waters, Mr Yang Yao Lin (楊耀林), Curator of the Shenzhen Museum, and the senior staff of the several Hong Kong Special Administrative Region (SAR) Government agencies listed below.

Specific acknowledgements for the colour and black-and-white illustrations are as follows: Hong Kong Museum of History, Figs. 1.1, 1.2, 5.1, and 5.2; Hong Kong Antiquities and Monuments Office, Plates 11, 13, and 23; Dr Anthony K. K. Siu, Plates 2, 3, 4, 5, 24, and 25; Dr David Faure, Figs. 2.3 and 2.5, and Plates 9 and 20; Dr Patrick Hase, Plates 16 and 22; Dr Betsy Johnson, Plate 19; Mr Yeung Pak-shing, Plates 10, 12, and 21; the Chan lineage of Cheung Kwan O, Fig. 2.2; Mr Chan Chik (陳迹), Fig. 3.4; Ken Haas, Plate 14; and Tim Ko Tim-keung, Figs. 1.3, 3.3, and 5.3. The Hong Kong Information Services Department kindly provided Plate 18, while its 1979 publication, *The Rural Architecture of Hong Kong* was the source of the plan at Fig. 3.1. The Lunar New Year couplet at Plate 6 was brushed by Mr Chan Wah-lun (陳華麟) of Hoi Pa New Village, Tsuen Wan, and Fig. 3.2 appeared in the *Lingnan Science Journal*, vol. 10, nos. 2 & 3, August 1931. The remaining illustrations are from my own photographs, or ones taken over the years by my colleagues in the former New Territories Administration, whilst Patrick Hase kindly drew the maps used as the basis for the Endpapers. Another friend, R. Ian Dunn of Sydney, has once more provided timely help and guidance in all matters photographic, including the front cover image, Endpaper maps, Fig. 4.4, and Plates 7 and 15.

I needed much help with finalizing this little book. My friends Valery and Richard Garrett of Hong Kong, May Holdsworth of Hong Kong, and Mariann Ford of Sydney all kept me going at several sticking points along the way, whilst Carey Vail—a superb editor of the sort who usually exists only in dreams—helped to clarify and improve the presentation at every step of the way with her incisive and helpful comments and suggestions, without affecting fundamentals. My heartfelt thanks to them all!

My dear wife Mabel Chiu-woon Wong (黃超媛) has ever provided maximum support for my compulsive writing. She has my eternal gratitude, and the book is dedicated to her with deep love and affection. I wish also to thank my late parents-in-law, Wong Kwan-pui (黃君沛) and Wong Chau Yuk-bing (黃周玉冰), ever mindful of their keen interest and help with my Chinese studies.

A Note on Romanization

When writing about Guangdong, or any other province of South China, it is necessary to use a combination of the predominant local language (in this case Cantonese) and pinyin in the text. Appropriateness to place and subject has been the guiding principle. Place names in the former British Crown Colony of Hong Kong are in Cantonese romanization, and follow the official publication, *A Gazetteer of Place Names in Hong Kong, Kowloon and the New Territories* (Government Printer, Hong Kong: 1960, and later reprintings), while place names in the Shenzhen municipality are given in pinyin, in line with Chinese national practice. Chinese characters provided in the Glossary should help to offset any problems with terms that are peculiarly Cantonese.

For my wife, Mabel Chiu-woon Wong

Introduction

There is no nation, numerically as great as China,
whose customs and modes of life are so generally common
to all parts of their vast empire
—Field Marshal Viscount Wolseley, 1903

THIS VOLUME IN the Images of Asia series describes traditional
village culture in South China. Specifically, it is about the
traditional village culture of Hong Kong and Shenzhen (see
Endpapers for relevant maps). Its contents were to be confined
originally to the Hong Kong villages, but now that the former
British Crown Colony is again part of China, a broader
approach is appropriate. Before 1841, the two areas were part
of the same county of Guangdong province. It is thus hardly
surprising that their settlements were not dissimilar in age
or size, that the population of each included both Cantonese
and Hakka speakers, and that the village culture was virtually
one and the same, besides sharing in the wider spectrum
mentioned in the opening quotation.

I lived and worked in Hong Kong for thirty-five years, and
have made frequent visits since moving residence in 1990.
For most of that time I was a civil servant, serving
periodically in the New Territories, in close touch with the
people, and directly involved in negotiating the removal and
resiting of villages for development, among them Shek Pik
on Lantau Island, which features prominently in this book.
I have had many conversations with the elderly about their
own family and village history, and have helped to collect
surviving documentation on traditional rural and family life,
along with items from their material culture. This was just
as well, since today's Hong Kong with its seven million

inhabitants is almost totally urbanized. Even surviving old villages have changed beyond recognition, whilst the true village economy, based on two rice crops annually, came to an end in the 1970s.

My acquaintance with the areas adjoining Hong Kong has been shorter, and necessarily less intensive. However, between 1980 and my retirement in 1987, my duties took me quite often into the then newly established Shenzhen Special Economic Zone; thereafter I made regular visits there, as well as to the neighbouring Baoan county, with friends from Hong Kong and from the Shenzhen Museum. I saw the countryside before it was overwhelmed by the torrent of development that is still spreading ever widely, but before very long, there was little to distinguish between the urbanized and industrialized areas on either side of the border. Following an adjustment of boundaries in 1993, Shenzhen municipality comprises both the Special Economic Zone and the former Baoan county. The new urban population now numbers over four million, instead of the 314,000 who lived there in 1979.

I have written other books on the rural communities of the Hong Kong region, but this volume takes more account of those broader aspects of village culture which are central to, and part of, the civilization of China. Confucian and non-Confucian elements alike take centre stage—with very good reason, since the evidence of this cultural conditioning is to be found everywhere around. It is little wonder that the Shenzhen Museum reminds its visitors that 'the historical culture [of the Shenzhen municipality] originates with both the common tradition of the Chinese nation and the local features of Shenzhen'. In Hong Kong and Shenzhen, as elsewhere in Guangdong province, these mainstream cultural elements provided an overarching and unifying framework that ordered villagers' social lives just as decisively as the seasons and the forces of nature determined their economic activities.

In the 1950s to 1970s, many leading Contemporary China specialists scrutinized Communist China intensively, but with little or no reference to the past. If we believe that the present era has no connection with what has gone before, we too are misjudging the situation. The old culture embodies much of the Chinese psyche and outlook, and despite loss of continuity since 1949, and a diminished understanding among many of the younger adult generation, it is still relevant for viewing Contemporary China. The eminent American historian F. W. Mote carries this view further, expressing his belief that 'ignorance of China's cultural tradition and historical experience is an absolute barrier to comprehending China today'. Nor can criticism be confined to Westerners: many years ago, addressing himself to Chinese authors who, in the first flush of enthusiasm about their nation's progress under Communism, were tending to denigrate their country's past, Dr Joseph Needham advised them gently that this was only to cut off the branch on which they were sitting.

Needless to say, I share these feelings. It is my sincere hope that this little book will help connect a lively past to the vibrant present in this small but significant part of China.

James Hayes
Sydney and Hong Kong
2000–2001

1
Hong Kong and Shenzhen: Xinan (New Peace) County

A veritable sea of mountains
—Revd Rudolph Krone, 1859

UPON CLIMBING A mountain in present day Shenzhen, the German missionary Rudolph Krone marvelled at 'the extended view' and was 'astonished at the barren masses of hills, constituting a veritable sea of mountains, which covers nearly the whole district'. He would also have seen that water was another principal element in the landscape, for the mainland areas were heavily indented by the Pearl River estuary and the South China Sea, with many islands in addition.

For those resident by or near the shore, coastal fishing was a major item in the local economy and almost as important as agriculture, itself everywhere in evidence (Fig. 1.1). Even in upland areas, every piece of land to which water could be led for rice cultivation was being exploited. Harvested in June–July and again in November–December, the rice crop was the principal livelihood of the majority of village people, and is so even today in outlying parts of the region (Plate 1). There were also many old-style rural industries—among them the operation of salt pans; the preparation of salt fish, fish paste, beancurd, soy sauce, and preserved fruits; the burning of coral and seashells for lime, brick-making, shipbuilding and repairing; stone quarrying; and leather manufacture. Oyster farming in Deep Bay was another distinctive local industry, conducted there for centuries.

1.1 A New Territories' valley in winter, *c.*1950 (courtesy of the Hong Kong Museum of History).

Before the onset of modern development, this area of southern China was extraordinarily beautiful. In every part of the region, vistas of mountain, sea, and sky gladdened the senses. Imagine, too, the once universal presence of the rice fields, with the young shoots standing in water during the growing periods of the year, and their mirror-like surfaces reflecting the passage of cumulus clouds across the sky.

There were also many people in the landscape. Unlike today, when the hill country is deserted, men and women were at work everywhere, in the hills as well as the plains, on the coastal flats and far inland. The land reflected the efforts made by their forebears to fashion it to their needs. Terraced fields with rubble stone walls, embankments along the coast, small dams and irrigation channels, the paved sections of upland footpaths, stone bridges, fishing stations overlooking the sea, and the like, all testified to generations of toil and infinite patience: a fact their descendants were prone to press upon Hong Kong government officials when having to give up their hard-won ancestral plots for development.

Local Settlements since the Song Dynasty

A diversity of size, layout, appearance, and ethnic composition characterized settlements across the region.[1] A full one thousand years of continuous residence is not uncommon in some places, but there are also villages and hamlets founded less than a century ago. Indeed, newcomers arrived to take up permanent residence in newly established or existing villages in each and every century. It is worth noting that entry to existing villages was not lightly given. It meant sharing resources; land and precious irrigation water in particular. Many lineages[2] relate how, unless establishing a new settlement, their first ancestor had to dwell outside the village of his choice for a considerable period before gaining entry.

3

Walled settlements were fairly common. Before the Second World War, the New Territories was estimated to contain twenty-three walled villages, and the number in Shenzhen could not have been less. In Hong Kong, the best known, and surely most photographed in the past for its romantic appearance, is Kat Hing Wai, one of the Deng lineage's seven old villages at Kam Tin (Fig. 1.2). A later walled village of spectacular appearance—but in a different style—Tsang Tai Uk at Sha Tin (Fig. 1.3), has few counterparts in Hong Kong, but more in Shenzhen (Plate 2). Many of these old settlements originally possessed moats, which together with their strong walls reflected the need for security in times past.

Sam Tung Uk in Tsuen Wan, now a museum, represents another type of village commonly found in the region. Of rectangular shape and regular layout, it had no walls, but its houses faced inward and presented only their windowless backs to the outside world. Security was again a consideration in a variation found in the Hakka areas of the New Territories. Here, the layout was essentially linear, with a central ancestral hall from which a corridor on each side, barred at the ends, divided the living accommodation into front and back dwellings. Yet, surprisingly enough, the great majority of villages were without walls or any kind of protection other than that afforded by their several rows of closely packed houses (Fig. 1.4).

Picturesque, solid, free-standing watchtowers of varying height are more numerous in Shenzhen and adjacent areas than in Hong Kong (Plate 1 shows a very modest example). Like the various walled villages, these watchtowers are yet another reminder of unsettled times. A few pagodas, structures of a different sort and purpose, still adorn the landscape; these were meant to improve the local geomancy

1.2 Kat Hing Wai, one of the Deng lineage's seven old villages at Kam Tin, in about 1930, when it still had its moat (courtesy of the Hong Kong Museum of History).

1.3 The walled village of Tsang Tai Uk, Sha Tin, Hong Kong, *c.*1970 (courtesy of Tim Ko).

1.4 The closely packed houses of Fan Pui village offered the only protection against the outside world, Lantau Island, 1957. Two years later, the residents were resited to a new village in the adjoining bay.

or *fengshui* (see Chapter 4), and with it the fortune of local scholars in the imperial examinations (Plate 3).

Then there were the market towns. Generally speaking, the right to set up a market was one given by the imperial government to prominent members of the larger lineages. Shenzhen Old Market was the most important in the region, rather larger than the other markets and one higher in the trading hierarchy. All followed the customary schedule of three marketing days in every ten, but since it was important for as many traders and clients as possible from all around to attend the Shenzhen market, other markets traded on different days. Mostly overtaken by development, few old market towns are recognizable today.

Among the imperial government centres of the region, the foremost was Nantou, a coastal defence office during the early Ming dynasty (1368–1644), and after 1573 the district city for the whole county of Xinan, or San On in Cantonese (Plate 24). Apart from its age, and the usual walls, gates, gatehouses, official buildings, and temples, Nantou's other claim to fame is that it had been stormed and captured from the sea by the British in 1858, during the Second Anglo–Chinese War. Among the rest of the government centres, the most celebrated was Kowloon Walled City,[3] opposite the island of Hong Kong, which although dating in its final appearance to 1847, had been an administrative centre since Song dynasty times (960–1279).

By the early twentieth century, long settlement, local conditions, and the genius of its people had produced a complex society, one which, to borrow the words of a leading historian of the region, 'notwithstanding the heavy mortality rates and overwhelming dominance of the economy by its primary producers typical of such a traditional society... shows us also the vigorous market towns and ports, and the complex life of a well-settled and confident, if small-scale and rural, community' (see Hase: 1996).

A Historical Perspective

Hong Kong and Shenzhen share memories of the Song period. There is the inscribed boulder of 1274 above the Tin Hau Temple in Hong Kong's Joss House Bay, the former Sung Wong Toi at Kowloon City, and other relics that recall the last days of the dynasty in and around this part of Guangdong, including the reputed grave of the last Song boy-emperor at Chiwan in Shenzhen. The Deng lineage of Kam Tin point proudly to the forebear who married a refugee princess of the Song imperial house (or, as some think, a member of another illustrious

7

family), the spirit tablets of both being kept to this day in the Ling Wan Nunnery below nearby Tai Mo Shan. The Wen clan of Shenzhen and the New Territories claims a connection with the Song patriot, poet, and chief minister, Wen Tianxiang (1236–1283), who died in prison in Beijing rather than serve the new Mongol dynasty of Kublai Khan.

The Shenzhen village of Sungang has existed from the early years of the Ming dynasty (1368–1644), founded by a man who loomed large in local and national history. He Zhen (1322–1388), made earl of Dongguan for his services in bringing Guangdong under the control of the new dynasty, served the first Ming emperor as a military commander and administrator. However, five years after his death, his younger brother and all but one of his own sons were executed by the suspicious emperor for their alleged involvement in the supposed treason of another military leader of the time. The tale is kept alive by the fanciful legends circulating in the region (see Page 10). The village is still located within the Shenzhen city suburbs (Plate 4).

Changes of dynasty usually brought unsettled times. Canton (Guangzhou) suffered terribly during the Ming–Qing changeover in the 1640s, and life over a huge area of Guangdong was disrupted by the new Manchu rulers' enforced Evacuation of the Coast in the years 1662–1669—thereby to deny aid to the Zheng family of Amoy and Formosa, which had continued to oppose the dynasty for forty years. Many families perished, and others did not return. After appeals made by both a viceroy and a governor of Guangdong moved the Emperor Kangxi to allow the people to return to their homes, a grateful populace built many memorial temples in the two men's honour. These include those at Kam Tin and Shek Wu Hui in the New Territories of Hong Kong, with two others at Nantou and Xixiang in Shenzhen.

Sea robbers and pirates were a periodic scourge, especially in the years 1790–1810, when large piratical fleets caused widespread havoc in the Canton Delta. Coastal dwellers themselves were not above resorting to piracy or receiving stolen goods. The region was also notorious for its inter-lineage and inter-village wars, sometimes conducted along ethnic lines. By the late nineteenth century, this area had long acquired a reputation for unruliness. 'The people are not lambs in the [New] Territory', a Hong Kong Governor asserted in the Legislative Council in 1910, to which a Chinese member of Council added an enthusiastic 'Hear! Hear!' Even as late as 1955, the District Commissioner of the New Territories had to negotiate an end to a vicious brawl between the men and boys of two Cantonese villages in the Yuen Long district, whose ancestors had been at odds for centuries, set off this time by a child who had innocently picked up a dead fish from the other village's fish pond. In 1959, another minor incident involving a cyclist and a pedestrian from opposing villages in the same area sparked an armed affray.

Before the Evacuation of the Coast most native inhabitants were Cantonese, but many Hakka people moved into the Xinan region thereafter. By 1898 their descendants probably accounted for nearly half the settled population, when the population of the whole county—less the indigenous boat people who lived and died afloat—was around 200,000. Originally from northern China, the Hakkas had gradually moved south in the centuries after the Mongol invasions of Song times. Speaking a language markedly different from Cantonese, and differing in some particulars in their customs, they were a hardy race who prided themselves on their strength and endurance, with many of the men engaging in the building and stonecutting trades.

Local Myth and Legend

Owing to its long history, the region is full of myth and legend. In Hong Kong, many local people and overseas visitors have heard of the Nine Dragons of Kowloon, whilst Castle Peak, Amah Rock above Sha Tin New Town, and Bride's Pool near Sha Tau Kok all feature in guidebooks and tourist literature for the New Territories. Less well known but equally interesting are what Revd Krone had styled 'locomotive rocks'. At Heung Shek near Chuen Lung village on Tai Mo Shan, the highest mountain in Hong Kong, intent upon improving the *fengshui* of the Tsuen Wan villages at its foot, three rocks were moving gradually down the slopes when they encountered a pregnant woman and could move no more. The local place name means Sounding Rocks, because one of them, when struck with a stone, produces a reverberating echo in the whole.

In the Sai Kung North area, four nearby islands are associated with an old legend about a noted courtier of the early Ming period who fell foul of his imperial master. The four locations were among thirty-six burial sites listed in a *fengshui* book (see Chapter 4) that came to the courtier 'from heaven', and would all be favourable to his descendants. However, this was considered to bode ill for the new dynasty. The emperor became suspicious and had the official decapitated. The story in its various forms has fanciful elements, but is tied into the saga of He Zhen, earl of Dongguan, and the fate of most of his family. Local legend has it that around the same time, and for similar reasons, the powerful Mao lineage settled near Yuen Long in the New Territories suffered the same fate at the hands of the emperor, and that the killings made the local stream run red with blood, giving rise to the place name Hung Shui Kiu or Red Water Bridge. The precise location of the old Mao village within the Hung Shui Kiu area is known to the elders of nearby villages to the present day.[4]

All major lineages across the county could provide a host of legends of different kinds, but few are recorded, one exception being those pertaining to the Deng lineage of Kam Tin, which were taken down and published pre-war. Some of the children's tales in the local languages incorporate legend and mythology. Needless to say, like legends everywhere, each tale has been subject to variation over the centuries.

Notes

1   I am excluding both pre-Song settlement, about which too little is known, and prehistory, on which much archaeological investigation has been carried out, with spectacular results (see Bard: 1988; *Collected Essays on the Culture of the Ancient Yue People in South China*: 1993; *Conference Papers on Southeast Asia*: 1995).

2   A lineage generally comprises the descendants of a founding ancestor in a particular place. A village can be single- or multi-lineage. This is a more precise definition than the term 'clan', which is more often used to describe a much looser social group, such as genealogically connected lineages living in different places (as in various counties of the same province), who may be able to trace their descent from the same distant ancestor, but have long since multiplied their settlements over many generations.

3   Kowloon Walled City was reopened in 1995 as a heritage park, well worth visiting, preserving the fully restored *yamen* set in Qing-style landscaping, some of the foundation stones from the original wall, and remnants of the South Gate.

4   For a discussion of these events and the legends to which they gave rise, see David Faure: 1986, pp. 149–50, 228 n. 2, 229–30 n. 11. Also, James L. Watson: 1991, pp. 165–9. Information keeps coming to light.

2
Shaping Village Culture:
Imperial Government and Local
Self-Management

Eighty percent or more of the Chinese population live their
daily lives under their customs, the common law of the
land, interpreted and executed by themselves
—H. B. Morse, 1908

As PUBLISHED IN 1908, Morse's dictum implies that the apparatus
of provincial and county government did not extend down to
the village level, and that local communities had largely to
look after themselves. This was in fact the case, and it provides
the key to understanding traditional village culture in the
closing years of the Qing dynasty (1644–1911).

Imperial Government

The Hong Kong region belonged to Xinan county, under the
charge of the county magistrate, whose *yamen* or official
office was located in the walled city of Nantou within
present-day Shenzhen. A few sub-county deputy magistrates
assisted him, with offices at different places, including
Kowloon Walled City.

Although the county magistrate's duties were wide, his
primary responsibilities were for maintaining peace and good
order in the countryside, and for securing the payment of
taxes for forwarding to higher authorities. To meet these
requirements, he had to rely heavily on the assistance and
cooperation of local leaders throughout the county.

Otherwise, the mandarins in general took little or no part in the management of towns and villages, nor the conduct of local affairs, and generally left people to their own devices. However their runners—or 'understrappers', as the missionary scholar Wilhelm Lobscheid styled them—were ruefully admitted by two famous reforming viceroys of the late nineteenth century to be 'the scourge of the people, in every province the same. It must be that the worst of the people take up this employment.' (See Note 3.)

Self-Management and Customary Law

Fortunately, local society was well organized for self-regulation and -management. Large and small alike, each lineage had its own managers, each village its elders and headman (Fig. 2.1), and each market town and coastal market centre its *kaifong* or committee. In addition, there were many

2.1 Mr Li Tam (born 1890), photographed in 1963, elder of Sheung Li Uk, one of the old villages of North-West Kowloon overtaken by development in the 1950s.

13

helpers—younger men assisting with various duties who one day would become elders and headmen in their turn.

Across the county, numerous alliances based on geographic location, lineage connections, and past history existed. In the New Territories alone, there were over twenty of these traditional linkages, including the quaintly named Double Fish Division, and the many others, styled *yue*, known only by designations of Four, Six, or Nine, and the like, their names derived from the varying numbers of the main participating villages. The origins of each remain shadowy, but go back centuries. Whatever their original purpose, by the late nineteenth century these alliances had become higher units in a self-management structure that embraced the lineages, villages, and market towns of the region. Their leading elders and gentry (Fig. 2.2) would come together to consult when necessary, and they would be summoned to meet the government officials when required.[1]

2.2 Chan Tak-hang (1828–1891), village leader, merchant of Kowloon City suburb, and gentry member with a purchased degree (courtesy of the Chan lineage of Cheung Kwan O, Junk Bay).

14

In such fashion, the whole burden of local management was borne by the leaders at various levels, operating through a corpus of customary law and practice administered by themselves. Petty crimes like stealing chickens and allowing cows to eat other folks' crops attracted fines; any injuries caused by fighting had to be compensated; and levies in cash or kind were imposed on households to meet the expenses of protective rituals.[2] At need, rules would be posted for public notice. With slight variations, the accepted local practices were known in each village and sub-district, bolstered as necessary by the threat of taking recalcitrants to the county magistrate's *yamen*, whilst magistrates would often enquire into local custom in the course of their judicial duties. Inside the village, each family's entitlements were given protection by the local custom; a good example being the recognition given to virtual ownership of the tracts of hillside where cattle were grazed and fuel cut for use or sale. Important assets in the family economy, these plots were loaned, transferred, mortgaged, or sold between villagers (but not to outsiders), though they might not possess legal rights of ownership. Village handbooks of the kind shown in Fig. 2.3 enshrined the multifarious local practices.

Village Justice

The customary law had many ramifications, but like the imperial statute law one of its principal features was that it imposed mutual responsibility for offences committed by members of the group, with the expectation of self-rectification. Selby, a Wesleyan missionary, once observed this in practice; in the course of a lengthy itineration from his mission station at Foshan near Canton in the 1870s, his personal possessions were stolen whilst he was taking a

禁耗盜田禾禁條式

為嚴禁耗盜田禾以靖風俗事功我鄉之人皆以務農為業具以既竭力

於東作庶有望於西成而上輸國課下給家人誠為朝廷草野之重事也

今有不良之徒專求利己不顧損人每當田禾成熟之際屢相盜竊兼之

牛馬鵝鴨踐食毀耗以致有耕無收國課難輸家人難給是實為人之

所切齒者茲特合眾嚴立禁規倘聞往來諸君倘有仍蹈前轍復

行耗盜無論當場捉獲與過後查出本族定合眾簽名送 官究

治決不寬貸自立禁以後各宜守法無貽後悔為可特此預

聞

本族裔全啟

2.3 A page from a village handbook in Fanling Wai, explaining that thieves caught stealing crops will be sent to the magistrate (courtesy of David Faure).

swim. Upon his complaint to the authorities, the matter was investigated by a council of local elders. 'In the afternoon', he wrote later, 'a solemn village council was held. Old tottering Enochs, and Methuselahs, and Abrahams, overshadowed by straw hats three-quarters of a yard in diameter, came riding in from the surrounding villages. They bore the same name and were mutually related by abstruse genealogical steps. After the council had met, I was told the theft would be further inquired into and my lost property should be restored next day.' As indeed it was.[3]

Community Duties

With government responsibility limited to its own primary concerns, local leaders and their assistants had plenty to do. Mediation always featured prominently. Judging by the evidence, settling quarrels and disputes took up much of their time, as there was always much potential for discord in village communities. Liaison with the civil and military authorities was another important task, along with the more unpleasant duty of negotiating with troublesome strangers who might arrive in their vicinity, such as robber bands or pirates and the commanders of foreign war vessels. They might also have had to mediate in inter-village and inter-lineage disputes.

In farming communities battling with the natural elements, making arrangements for the performance of various community rituals that were the norm in village life formed a regular part of the leaders' work. At the beginning and end of each lunar year, services of supplication and thanksgiving, respectively, had to be performed at one of the earth god shrines of the locality. This was a practice often shared between groups of villages worshipping together at the same shrine. Other regular rituals were also required, together with what may be styled those 'occasional' ones needed in an emergency to combat or neutralize perceived threats to the health and safety of the community. Then again, after an especially good harvest, or in celebration of their temple god's annual birthday, the leaders might have to hire itinerant players or a puppet troupe to perform operas (intended more for the gods than the people) as part of the thanksgiving celebrations. Such events were highly enjoyable, full of life and colour. An essential part of village culture, these rituals and celebrations provided an important unifying element—culture and community being indivisible.

The financing of these events was shared and obligatory, and provided by subscription. At Shek Pik village in the 1920s, the levy had been one Hong Kong dollar per adult male and fifty cents per male child, with a catty (0.67 kilogram) of rice on cows and half a catty on calves. At need, the levies would be topped up with donations by better-off villagers. For their part, managers were accountable, and statements of income and expenditure had to be posted for public scrutiny (Fig. 2.4). In the case of temple repairs, the names of all donors were to be recorded on commemorative tablets. Slackness led the organizers of an 1896 temple repair at Tai O, Lantau, to make the following shamefaced admission, the nervousness of the wording underlining a keen recognition of their public duty: 'On this stone tablet appear the names of many but not all the donors. At this late date, it has been like groping in the dark for pearls. Some are bound to be missed. Forgetting a few names is perhaps inevitable but if there has been any omission it is not intentional and should be pardoned.'

The managerial posts were undoubtedly arduous. Local people had a volatile nature, with marked tendencies to theatrical exaggeration. They were belligerent folk too, made so by having to be self-reliant and cope with emergencies.

2.4 Lists of subscribers to the opera performance and ritual opening of the newly resited Hung Shing Temple are pasted to the wall; Fan Pui New Village, 1959. The smaller notice on the left lists donations from expatriates working on the Shek Pik reservoir.

The usual response to the unusual and unexpected was to summon all villagers by frenzied gonging and drumming. The leaders were in many, if not most, cases only *primus inter pares*; their authority being dependent upon community assent, they could at times be quite powerless.

Shared Government

The political and social culture of the late Qing dynasty was embedded in the villages. Reaching outwards and upwards, and in effect a meshing of central authority and local power, it was both effective and impressive, contributing much to the stability of the imperial state. Two important forces underpinned the whole structure of government and society. As pointed out by S. Wells Williams (1848), the educational

19

system provided 'a full understanding of the principles on which officials are to govern'. All who had pursued the same course of study—in effect, all who had received the same instruction and indoctrination—would have had this basic understanding. This included the common people, to whom this awareness was communicated through an education of varying length, mostly short, but also by upbringing and supplementary instruction, and even through the overall village environment. This shared experience provided the essential link between the rulers and the ruled.

The second factor was equally important. The men who served as local leaders were undoubtedly capable. Whatever they were doing, they would have known what to do and how to do it, and they would have built up a fund of knowledge about local people and the local scene. Anyone privileged to watch their successors at work in recent times could see that management was, so to speak, 'in their blood'. Even as late as the 1970s and 1980s, during research in the Hong Kong villages, David Faure was able to assess the character and calibre of these modern counterparts and, like this author, challenge the view that leadership in late-Qing China came only from the gentry: 'If you walk around and have to ask your way about', he wrote, 'it dawns on you that the chap who guides you through all these things is not just a pawn in the system, oppressed under some rigid rules controlled by some outside force. You get to see him as a free agent in his own right and to know something of his social, religious and economic behaviour.'

A further element in the equation was the calibre of the people themselves. They possessed what that tough egg, the nineteenth century British consul Harry Parkes, called 'their own governable character' when accounting for the smooth administration of Canton and its one million inhabitants by an Anglo–French–Chinese commission in the course of nearly four years' occupation by the two foreign powers in 1858–61. Whilst hardly appropriate for all, it did apply to the bulk of the population.

A Written Village Culture

Finally, self-management in the villages and sub-districts was founded upon a literary capability. The limitations and shortfalls of rural education notwithstanding, the amount of documentation used in everyday life was impressive, its content extending into most areas of social and economic activity. Land was the most precious asset in the village, minutely divided up among the village families. The rice fields were generally very small, and there were a great many of them. At Shek Pik alone, there were over 4,000 agricultural plots to 400 house lots. Fields especially were frequently changing hands by sale and mortgage (Fig. 2.5). There as elsewhere in the region, it would seem that all such transactions were recorded in writing, whilst genealogical and other records indicate that the writers were usually people from the same lineage or village as the sellers. Model formats were always to hand through the practice of passing on old deeds for the same land to the latest purchasers, and exemplars for this and other kinds of documentation, existing in both manuscript and printed form, provided the written protocols for the social underpinning of the village and lineage, and were used in connection with adoptions, betrothals, marriages, funerals, and the like. For these, too, writers were usually available, some able to provide the couplets and other ephemera needed at the Lunar New Year, as well as on other occasions (Plates 5 and 6).

2.5 Deed of sale for rice fields at Shek Pik, dated 1831 (courtesy of David Faure).

The production of charms and the chanting of protective rituals belonged to a field that was mostly left to the professionals, usually Daoist or Buddhist priests or practitioners. However, a few village men were also competent in this field, having either inherited such skills or developed an expertise (see Fig. 4.4). Being mysterious and beyond most people's ken, their manuscript books were sometimes, out of fear, burned or discarded after their deaths in cases where the deceased practitioner had no apprentices. The many elders versed in Chinese herbal medicine also kept manuscript or printed books, and at a rather higher literary level, the more educated men of the locality might join together in poetry clubs.[4]

The village schoolmaster—often a man of modest background from the same or an adjoining settlement, who would spent his whole life in the service of education—was another useful prop to the system. In the smaller villages, he was very ready to assist, adding to his income (as noted by one observer in 1902) 'by acting as letter-writer for the village, by telling fortunes, by writing ornamental scrolls with which the Chinese delight to adorn their houses, and if he has ability for it, by writing petitions or complaints for presentation to the mandarins in lawsuits'—but, as I have been told, 'not always requiring money for his services, since small gifts in kind and invitations to marriage feasts and the like sufficed by way of recognition'. For an example of the skills of a village schoolmaster, see Plate 12, which shows the fine couplets brushed for his own ancestral hall by Teacher Hu of Ma On Kong, Pat Heung, New Territories, and transferred in gold onto heavy red-painted camphor-wood boards.[5]

The management and regulation of local society and the flourishing of village culture were grounded on such capabilities. The rural schools played a crucial role.[6] So long as they could turn out a sufficient number of more or less literate people to carry out the everyday work of the community, together with a few men of greater attainments to give style and distinction to the rest, village society could be carried on effectively and indefinitely, without the need for assistance or intervention from the state. By and large, this was achieved in our region.

Notes

1   Besides these purely indigenous leaders, there were other local persons who performed certain functions on behalf of the administration, but were not themselves officials or government employees. These included *dibao*, or rural agents, appointed by and answerable to the district magistrate and his subordinates, and to others with responsibilities in connection with fiscal matters like land registration and tax collection. However, these posts and their holders scarcely feature in local records, nor in old people's recollections of the late nineteenth century.

2   These examples are taken from the Shek Pik valley on Lantau Island, whose inhabitants were removed and resited for construction of a major reservoir in 1959–60. During my work there, I obtained much information from the elders on their social organization and history, some of which is included in this Chapter and elsewhere. For more details, see Chapter 4 of my book, *The Hong Kong Region*: 1977.

3   Thomas Selby (*Chinamen at Home*: 1900) was witness to the venality of the county administration: 'The local police authorities took a hand after the articles had been restored. They created difficulties for the elders and the clan that led to recurrent "squeezing" of cash.' Proverbs attest to the wisdom of not providing opportunities for official intervention in local affairs.

4   Patrick Hase (1990) has provided a most useful illustrated account of the work and interests of village scholars, based on his retrieval of several manuscript collections from the New Territories for public consultation and enjoyment.

5   The names of the artisans who made such transfers onto more enduring materials—work probably undertaken in Canton or some other urban centre—are, sadly, hardly ever recorded.

6   Nonetheless, the majority of skills needed on the farm and at home would be learned by emulation, and not in school, and by relying on the few for indispensable documentation as and when required, many villagers would soon forget what they had learned there. See also Hase (1990) for what he styles 'teaching songs'.

3

The Confucian Imprint:
Instruction and Indoctrination in the Village

The classics, which are read and learned by heart from
beginning to end, treat of filial piety and political economy,
so that China must always abound in dutiful children
and excellent governors
—Revd Charles Gutzlaff, 1834

TONGUE IN CHEEK as this may be, Gutzlaff's dictum contains
an eternal truth, for there can be no doubt that the ordinary
Chinese impressed many Westerners at that time and before.
Besides Harry Parkes' praise recounted in Chapter 2, Sir John
Davis, formerly of the East India Company's Select
Committee at Canton, and one of the early governors of the
British Crown Colony of Hong Kong, had accorded to what
he styled 'the Chinese lower classes' the accolade that they
'were better educated or at least better trained than in most
other countries'.

It is usual to ascribe this trait and training to the Confucian
ethos that permeated Chinese life for so long and continuous
a period of the national existence. The central tenet of
Confucius' teachings was that the proper ordering of human
relationships through instruction would lead to good
behaviour by the individual and good government by the ruler;
part of what F. W. Mote calls 'the search for order in a turbulent
world' on which Confucian political thought turned.
Eighteenth-century Europeans had been duly impressed,
among them the English poet Alexander Pope, who captured
its essence in one of his peerless couplets: 'Superior and alone
Confucius stood/Who taught that useful science—to be good.'

Confucianism in the Countryside

Frederick Mote has also commented that 'Every Chinese, educated or illiterate, growing up on the *Analects* as a text to be studied or as the common stuff of daily speech, has felt perhaps as if he lived with Confucius peering over his shoulder.' This is certainly the impression I received during my early years of government service in Hong Kong, when I had much to do with the people of the 180 old villages under my care.

This was further reinforced by closer acquaintance with one particular village, Shek Pik on Lantau Island (see Chapter 4). Among the many indications available there as to the extent of Confucianization was a woodblock edition of the *Analects*, passed to me by a villager, which had belonged to his grandfather. From the red dots that were used to mark off sentences throughout, probably by the schoolmaster, it was clear that the boy had been through the whole text, and had no doubt been required to commit it to memory (Plate 7).

Confucianism had begun to reach down to the common people in the Song dynasty (960–1279) through the spread of education and printed books, the influence of scholar-officials, the adoption of forms of ritual practice hitherto confined to the elite, and the reordering of Confucian texts and teachings by the neo-Confucian scholar and publicist Zhu Xi (1130–1200). However, the coverage was not due solely to indoctrination from above and imitation from below. Patricia Ebrey thinks that the evolution of a patrilineal and patriarchal family structure throughout Chinese society was at least equally responsible for fostering the practice of filial submission, which in its wider applications was for so long such a key element in the ideology of the imperial state.

This reasoning is especially relevant for Guangdong province, the land of lineages, with a very well-developed lineage structure among its people. Large and small, they could number a few tens of people of the same name living on their own in a tiny hamlet or along with other lineages in a bigger settlement, or run into many thousands living in a large village or group of villages. On the plentiful evidence available on all sides, there can be no doubt whatsoever of the relevance of Confucianism for the village culture of the region.[1]

Ancestral Halls

It had long been the practice of the larger Cantonese lineages to erect 'halls of ancestors' in which, through the performance of rites at fixed times of the year, their male members could venerate the founders and the sons or grandsons who established branches in the place of settlement. In Hong Kong and Shenzhen, many of these imposing structures date from the eighteenth century, and some are older still (Plate 8, and Fig. 3.1). The halls were associated with what were called lineage trusts (*zu*, or *tang*), managed by elders, and endowed with land for their upkeep and to maintain the sacrifices.

Ancestral halls were the social and religious hub of the lineage. They contained the soul tablets of ancestors of past generations, and the genealogical records were often kept there for safekeeping. The serried ranks of green and gold tablets still to be seen in some of the larger halls in the New Territories are an impressive sight (Plate 11). Researching in the Liao lineage village of Sheung Shui in the 1960s, Hugh Baker was moved to comment: 'The strong accent on ancestor worship and memorialism indicates how heavily the living lineage leans on its dead forbears.'[2]

Section 截面圖

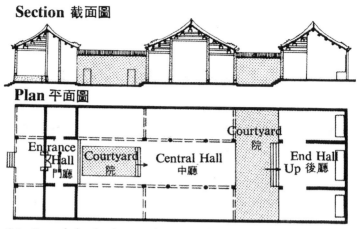

Plan 平面圖

3.1 Ground plan for the west-facing Liao lineage ancestral hall, Liao Wanshitang, with three halls and an enclosed courtyard in front, believed to date from 1751 (courtesy of the Hong Kong Information Services Department).

Crucial to the wellbeing of a major lineage was the production of scholars who could take the imperial examinations and obtain official rank and senior positions in the administration—for government service was the principal highway to riches and influence. Ancestral halls were invariably schoolrooms, and their landed property provided the means to educate boys and engage fine teachers. The genealogies of the major lineages of the region show considerable numbers of degree holders, by examination (*kejiaban*) or more often by purchase (*juanban*).

A large lineage with scholar-officials and degree men was part of the Establishment of imperial China. Outwardly, an ancestral hall demonstrated wealth and power, and its fittings confirmed this impression. These included the honour boards of clansmen who had been successful in the imperial examinations (Plate 13), and the graduates' flagpoles placed between granite slabs in front of the halls to proclaim their achievements (Fig. 3.2). There might also be a number of *biane*, the elegant decorated boards bearing calligraphic inscriptions presented by fellow-provincials holding high office, or provided by them upon request.

Yet ancestral halls were not meant only for the educated and powerful members of a lineage. The majority of its members might be ordinary farmers tilling fields owned by the lineage trusts, but it is clear from local records that all males were included in the spring and autumn rituals to honour the ancestors, including the distribution of sacrificial pork that accompanied the event.

The spread of Confucian beliefs is made yet more manifest through the small ancestral halls of the lesser lineages of the region, Cantonese and Hakka alike, but particularly among

3.2　Graduates' flagpoles proudly erected outside an ancestral hall, Honam Island, Canton, *c.*1920 (courtesy of *Lingnan Science Journal*).

the latter. Though less obtrusive, and without their connotations of wealth and power, there were many more of the smaller ancestral halls than larger buildings of the major lineages. Some were free-standing structures, albeit of simpler design and proportions (Plate 9). However, the great majority were located within the several long rows of houses of the ordinary village and were scarcely distinguishable from the houses on either side. The honour boards of non-kin scholar-officials of the same family name could also be found there, shedding a reflected glory and hinting at influence in high places.[3]

Gratitude for past assistance is a Confucian ethic that is highly developed and can extend over many generations. In one of the Tsuen Wan villages, standing side by side with the He lineage ancestral hall, is another, dedicated to a person from the area who assisted the founding ancestor and gave him his daughter to wed. Both halls had to be reprovisioned from the old village when it was resited to make way for development (Plate 10). Such halls, together with a few old graves of non-kin being maintained by some lineages, show this particular Confucian ethic in action at the village level.

Ancestral Graves

It has long been the custom to build formal graves for founding ancestors. The large grave of one of the Deng lineage of Kam Tin on a small hill outside my District Office in Tsuen Wan had been placed there in the year 1100. The practice spread, and by the eighteenth century such graves were being provided for many people, female as well as male, as demonstrating expected duty and filial piety. They were expensive to build, and the services of a geomancer were always required.

30

In Hong Kong, despite many removals to make way for modern development, old graves are still commonly found in the hills and undeveloped parts of the region (see Fig. 4.1). Their very number is impressive, and their often strikingly beautiful locations lend themselves to pondering the past. Each grave has one or more tablets commemorating the deceased, stating its date and whether it is the original construction or has been repaired.

Worship at the grave site was as important as the general worshipping ceremonies that took place in the ancestral halls, and was carried out in the spring and autumn; by the late Qing dynasty (1644–1911) it was accompanied by much formality in large lineages, with a master of ceremonies and men wearing long gowns, marshalled and worshipping in strict accordance with generation and age. Only men and boys could participate then: informality and participation by all family members is the rule nowadays (Plate 14).

Genealogies

Genealogies are the records of the lineages. In the New Territories, Shenzhen, and adjoining areas, the majority of small lineages had manuscript rather than printed genealogies. Manuscript genealogies vary a good deal. Some list only recent branch descent; others carry the record back many centuries, or even over millennia to a mythical past. Some are detailed, others are not; or else detail is available for some generations but not for others. Their length and interest for the historian varies according to the zeal of their compilers, the materials open to him, and the accidents of time.

Many records include materials showing a strong Confucian flavour. The genealogy of the Xu lineage of Shek

Pik, besides quoting from Confucius and the *Book of Poetry* on filial piety, lists the rules drawn up by an ancestor of the eighteenth generation of the main line (who lived about 1600) for worship at the lineage's tombs in the adjacent home county of Dongguan, which the Shek Pik founder had left about 1475 to establish his new home.

Instruction at School and Home

The backbone of Confucian instruction was the village (or lineage) school. The schoolmaster, the texts in use, and the mode of teaching were its primary elements. The books studied were the Chinese classical texts: the *Four Books* and the *Five Classics* for bright boys who spent years at school, and simpler texts like the *Trimetric Classic* for those who only had a few years' education. Each child studied at his own pace, and it was the practice for students to bawl out their lessons individually, occasionally being summoned forward to 'back the book', in other words to recite passages correctly from memory. The extent of literacy in village populations appears to have varied, but in our region in the late nineteenth century, it was more usual than not for boys to have received a few years' instruction in the side rooms of ancestral halls, temples, or school buildings.

Confucius was paramount as the sage, the fount of learning. His likeness was in every schoolroom, and incense was burned in front of it every morning. At Shek Pik, the headman recalled, boys had taken this duty in turn. On the day he began school, he had been taken first to worship at the village temple, and had then to bow before Confucius and to his teacher in the classroom. School began at 6 a.m.

or earlier. Breakfast was taken at 9 a.m., and lunch at 12 noon. Study continued until late afternoon. The only breaks were at planting and harvest times, when boys were required to help on the farm, and at the Lunar New Year and some other major festivals.

The moral and instructive aspects of teaching were the most important elements in the whole educational system. To know what was universally recognized and accepted to be right conduct, and to be properly acquainted with protocol and ritual, were *the* thing. The family was, of course, the obvious place to start. Social etiquette was part of a child's upbringing (see Page 77). The prescribed forms of address—both highly specific and varied—used towards seniors and juniors of both sexes, inside and outside the family, had to be known and practised, often under the watchful eyes of a grandmother. No one who has heard mothers requiring their children to greet adults can doubt the intensity of past training. As if to crown the edifice, the number of phrases in common use that were drawn from the Chinese Classics was surprisingly large.[4]

The easy courtesy shown to me by villagers upon entering their homes during my rural visits as a young District Officer in the 1950s, which impressed me so much at the time, could most certainly be attributed to generations of training in the Confucian niceties.

Instruction through the Arts

However, the schoolroom and the home were far from being the only places where Confucian-based instruction was imparted.

Dance Troupes

In practically every village there would be a lion dance troupe and instructor. Most young men received this form of instruction, which included proper behaviour, as well as the niceties and etiquette of dance and its musical accompaniment. Stress was laid on the Confucian virtues, and on patience and forbearance. Whilst encouraged to be spirited and courageous, signs of temper were sternly put down. Interestingly enough, the dance sequences had to be as equally 'proper' as did conventional human relationships. There was, for instance, a right way and a wrong way for a 'lion' to enter and leave a temple, and the correct steps to take upon meeting another 'lion' and its instructor. Training in martial arts also featured in the curriculum, since defence of the village was the ultimate duty. In Hakka villages, the dancing creature was always a unicorn, the masks used for lions and unicorns being quite different from each other, as were some elements of the dance.

In the past, these troupes performed many important duties, including ceremonial functions of all kinds. They might be called upon to greet important visitors to the village, accompany a bride to her new home, celebrate the opening of a new home or shop, parade round the village during protective rituals and at festival times, accompany the portable image of the local temple deity to its place of honour in a theatrical matshed,[5] or escort ancestral tablets into a new ancestral hall, to name only some of these occasions (Fig. 3.3).

Manuscript and Printed Exemplars

Guidance in the protocol and formats used in connection with births, marriages, respected old age, death, and commemoration was available in manuscript exemplars. A

3.3 A unicorn dance to celebrate a wedding in the village of Ngau Tau Kok, Kowloon, 1960 (courtesy of Tim Ko).

sufficient number of such 'books' has survived to show that they were an important means of information transmission in the villages. Largely the province of schoolmasters and literate elders, they were copied and recopied by promising pupils and passed around, ensuring continuity of knowledge with expertise. Many printed books also dealt with these topics, some of them providing extensive coverage.

The Almanac, Novels, New Year Pictures, and Cigarette Cards

The ubiquitous annual almanacs, with their miscellanies of potted culture, were another means to continue indoctrination and remind of instruction. Printed or hand-copied novels and stories were also to be found in some village homes, mostly carrying a strong didactic message, as well as providing entertainment. The pictures that were produced for the Lunar

New Year, meant to be hung or pasted up in people's houses, were another vehicle for instruction and indoctrination, and by the early twentieth century, cigarette cards in large quantities further augmented the stock of such materials (Plate 15). This list of categories is not exhaustive.

Storytellers and the Theatre

For those who could not read, or did so only with difficulty, some elders of the village were always keen to pass on the old tales received from their forebears. There were also occasional visits from professional storytellers, a class of people renowned for both their repertoires and their narrative skills. The theatre was another major source of instruction and information for village audiences. In Xinan county as elsewhere in China, itinerant troupes of either actors or puppeteers were hired to perform at temple festivals, or on special occasions. Cantonese and Hakka troupes of each type were available, while the stock of historical tales was largely shared. Performances exerted a powerful hold upon what were, until recently, mostly standing, open-air audiences (Fig. 3.4). Their impact was such that, together with the famous novels of the past, the great and ever popular social dramas and historical epics of the Chinese theatre were considered by one authority of the time to be 'by far more influential organs of education than the schools and the literary examinations'.[6]

Instruction through Vernacular Architecture

The vernacular architecture of Xinan county was rich in decoration (see Knapp: 1999, 2000; Lung: 1991; *Rural*

1. The second rice crop, Jiulongshan, Huidong, 1998.

2. Walled village of Lungtianshiju at Pingshan, Shenzhen, 1994 (courtesy of Anthony K. K. Siu).

3. The Wen lineage pagoda, Fuyong, Shenzhen (courtesy of Anthony K. K. Siu).

4. Sungang walled village, Shenzhen, 1987 (courtesy of Anthony K. K. Siu).

5. The author standing beside a Lunar New Year couplet—wishing the occupants sufficient clothing, good food, and fine wine—pasted on the doorway of a house in Gushu village, Shenzhen, 1993 (courtesy of Anthony K. K. Siu).

6. Laudatory couplet, likening the author to two ancient Chinese worthies, brushed by his friend Mr Chan Wah-lun, Hoi Pa New Village, Tsuen Wan.

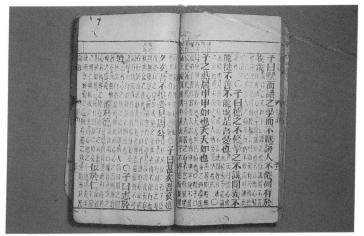

7.   A page from a boy's Confucian *Analects*, marked with red dots by the teacher. Born in Shek Pik in 1866, the boy in question became a teacher, herbal doctor, and writer of charms and documents, in the time-honoured pattern of bright village youths.

8.   The recently renovated Liao Wanshitang at Sheung Shui in 1986, dating from 1751.

9. Small ancestral hall in the village of Guoyuanshiju, showing signs of neglect after decades of Communist rule when such buildings were put to other uses, Pingshan, Shenzhen, 1990 (courtesy of David Faure).

10. Confucian gratitude: memorial hall (right) to the man who helped the He lineage's first ancestor, beside the He ancestral hall at Muk Min Ha New Village, Tsuen Wan, both reprovisioned from the old village when it was resited for development (courtesy of Yeung Pak-shing).

11. Altar with ancestral tablets, Liao Wanshitang. Made of wood, each tablet is enclosed within a wooden sleeve, often decorated with raised characters and painted in red or green and gold, each bearing the name of a male or female ancestor. Females honoured in this way were usually the wives of the lineage's founder, or of the sons who established the branches of the lineage (courtesy of the Hong Kong Antiquities and Monuments Office).

12. Altar of the Hu lineage ancestral hall, Ma On Kong, northern New Territories. The large couplets on wooden boards, in praise of the family, were written by a schoolmaster (born 1880) belonging to the lineage (courtesy of Yeung Pak-shing).

13. Honour tablets (*biane*) of successful examination candidates from the Deng lineage, at Wing Lung Wai, Kam Tin (courtesy of the Hong Kong Antiquities and Monuments Office).

14. Ancestral grave of the Chen lineage of Sam Tung Uk, Tsuen Wan (copyright Ken Haas, 1979).

15. Two of the twenty-four examples of filial piety shown on cigarette cards: a son melts the ice to catch fish for his parents, and a son seeks and eventually finds his mother, probably from the 1920s or 1930s.

fung shui line

16. Correcting *fengshui*: Lung Shan Temple at Lung Yeuk Tau, northern New Territories, 1993. As recommended by a geomancer, the ruined Lung Kai Nunnery was rebuilt to seven storeys as the Lung Shan Temple, in order to offset adverse geomantic forces that stemmed from the redevelopment of the area (courtesy of Patrick Hase).

17. A temporary shrine placed at a building site in Tung Chung in 1980, now the location of Hong Kong's international airport and Tung Chung New Town. The shrine's purpose was to placate the local earth gods following disturbance of the ground for site formation.

18. Carrying an 86-year-old lady from Shek Pik at the village removal in 1960. Inspector Pat Nash of the Marine Police supervises his men charged with aiding the family, watched by her grandson (courtesy of the Hong Kong Information Services Department).

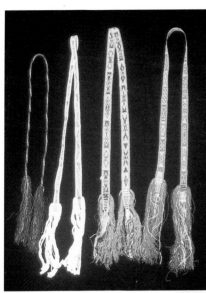

19. Patterned bands woven by Hakka women, used as straps for headgear, aprons, and the like, Tsuen Wan, 1970s (courtesy of Betsy Johnson).

20. A 76-year-old former *san po tsai*, or 'little daughter-in-law', at Pingshan, Shenzhen, with the author (courtesy of David Faure).

21. Women worshippers at Sai Chuk Lam Buddhist Nunnery, Tsuen Wan, 1996 (courtesy of Yeung Pak-shing).

22. Recently renovated Deng Ancestral Hall, Lung Yeuk Tau (courtesy of Patrick Hase).

23. Renovated Kan Ting Study Hall, Ping Shan, New Territories (courtesy of the Hong Kong Antiquities and Monuments Office).

24. Renovated guardhouse over an old city gate at Nantou, 1999 (courtesy of Anthony K. K. Siu).

25. The rebuilt Tianhou Temple at Chiwan, Shenzhen, 1999 (courtesy of Anthony K. K. Siu).

3.4 The open-air audience at a Cantonese opera performance remains enthralled, despite the rain, Tai O, 1958 (courtesy of Chan Chik).

Architecture in Hong Kong: 1979, 1989; *The Living Building*: 1995). Mural paintings, sententious calligraphy carved above doorways and corridors, representations of scenes from history and legend in carved and painted wood on the crossbeams, together with devices and decoration in stucco and stone, were found on and inside many of the better village structures. Some derived from Confucian texts, others from Buddhist and Daoist imagery: all were intended to be didactic or auspicious. The temples were especially noteworthy for their extensive use of the coloured tiles and pottery figures and creatures made in the Shiwan kilns near Canton. Even the very modest one in the abandoned Shek Pik Old Village had its leaping carp (symbol of successful scholarship with official rank), and pearl-like orb (symbol of good augury) upon its roof (see Fig. 4.2).

Part of the wider decorative tradition, the symbolism used in Chinese art and architecture has been described by Arthur Hummel in the following terms: 'China's art is an unconscious reflection of a people's way of life: their hopes, ambitions, their inmost desires. Her artists and writers—more than in most countries—were sustained by moral and ethical ideas. They found that symbols served best when referring to things timeless and eternal. We miss these intentions, however, if we gloss over what the symbols say.' Nor must we forget the auspicious couplets, lucky papers, and door gods at every village doorway, in one or other shade of vermilion-red, the colour of happiness and good fortune, all with their direct or derived meanings (Plate 5).

Buttressed in so many ways, it is hardly surprising that Confucianism had reached down to the masses. This was certainly the verdict of Dr Arthur H. Smith, author of the classic work *Village Life in China* (1896), who described the degree of permeation achieved among all classes of people in the following terms: 'The certainty that this is the best system of human thought as regards the relations of man to man is as much a part of the thinking of every educated Chinese as his vertebrae are a part of his skeleton'; adding *'and the same may be said of the uneducated Chinese, when the word feeling is substituted for thinking'* [author's italics].

Notes

1 Yet, as David Faure shows in his 1986 study of the lineages and villages of the New Territories of Hong Kong *as institutions*, the institutionalization of the lineage came relatively late, in a process that 'filtered downwards from the richer to the poorer villages over four centuries' (from the sixteenth century on). Whilst this institutionalization greatly strengthened the Confucian imprint on the countryside, it was far from originating solely with Zhu Xi and later neo-Confucianist influences—other components being territorial worship, rights of settlement and landholding,

building alliances, and acquiring official recognition. The impact of neo-Confucianism upon some much older features of the lineage and village is shown by Chan Wing-hoi (*The Journal of the Hong Kong Branch of the Royal Asiatic Society*, 36 (1996), pp. 107 seq.).

2   The intensity of ancestral worship in the lineage was neither uniform nor consistent, but neither is humankind. Ancestral halls were not always kept in good repair, nor used by all branches of a lineage. Quarrels and feuds of diverse origin could stand in the way, whilst superstition or adverse *fengshui* could sometimes lead to their being shunned—as was also the case with some village temples and graves.

3   This practice (for such it was) serves to confirm what the elders of one old village advised me was the long-held conviction that you did not need to seek protection from the deities if you had an official in your lineage. However, this did not stop villagers from resorting to all possible means of securing protection (see Chapter 4).

4   J. Dyer Ball (1905) devoted a volume to phrases in common use from the *Four Books*, and had another ready for publication on those in the *Five Classics*. Appendix A of F. W. Baller's *An Analytical Chinese–English Dictionary*, first issued for the China Inland Mission in 1900, consists of 'Selected passages from the *Four Books* and *Standard Commentary of Chu-hsi*'.

I myself chose a common proverb for the title page of my memoirs, *Friends and Teachers* (1996), without realizing at the time that it came from the *Analects*, or that Joseph Needham had also given it pride of place in the preliminary pages of *Clerks and Craftsmen in China and the West* (Cambridge: Cambridge University Press, 1970). The proverb roughly translates as, 'If I walk along with two others, one or other of them will certainly be able to teach me something.'

5   The traditional matshed was a temporary structure, sometimes very large, made of lashed bamboo poles, covered with mats.

6   Hu Shi, the Republican scholar largely responsible for the replacement of the age-old 'book language' with the *baihua* or spoken language, called the novels 'the Classics of the people', from which 'the vast populace have been learning practical wisdom, morals, manners, speech, glimpses of history, religion, humor and superstition'.

4

Non-Confucian Belief and Practice

*To we men of Tang [i.e. Cantonese] fengshui
is crucial*

THESE WORDS OF an elderly villager of Lantau Island said to me in 1961 convey the strength and feeling behind this most widespread and ingrained conviction among the rural folk of the region. But it was left to a well-informed Westerner to be more specific, even blunt. In his classic work, *The Middle Kingdom* (1848), the nineteenth-century American missionary-scholar-diplomat S. Wells Williams averred that *fengshui* was 'a source of terror', which seems to have been true enough in his day.

Fengshui

Fengshui was the term applied to the general geomantic quality of a locality. 'Good *fengshui*' was secured by the auspicious siting of villages, houses, temples, graves, and similar human constructions on the surface of the earth. The men who determined *fengshui* (I have not yet come across a female geomancer) were styled *di shi* or 'experts in land', or more generally as *fengshui xiansang* or 'teachers of *fengshui*'.

The practice of *fengshui* was called *di xue* or 'land learning'. One of its two principal branches was concerned with the dwellings of the living; the other with the abodes of the dead, whether in burial urns enclosed within formal graves, or simply in urns placed on the bare hillsides (Fig. 4.1).

4.1 Old grave mound with burial urns placed nearby to share in its good *fengshui*, hillside at Shek Pik, Lantau Island, 1958.

A grave was often referred to by village people as a *fengshui*. Providing auspicious sites for their tombs had become an integral part of ancestral worship, though its purpose was far from altruistic. A letter sent to my District Office in the early 1960s about the graves of a lineage put it very plainly: 'Ancestral worship has the dual purpose of appeasing the [souls of the] dead, and ensuring that the living flourish and prosper.'

The selection of sites was, and is, done by using the *luopan* or geomancer's compass.[1] The most complex of these comprise as many as 36 concentric circles, within which all the various sets of figures, characters, and elements employed in calculating good and bad influences are set out. The study of *fengshui* goes back into the mists of Chinese antiquity: a book written in the fourth century BC gives burial rules and makes geomantic comments. The notion that the ancestors could bring good or bad fortune to their descendants is also of ancient origin, and became linked to the study of graves at an early date. Countless printed books and manuscripts have been written on these major topics over two millennia and more.

The Impact of Fengshui at Village Level

Villagers as a body were always concerned lest changes in, or human interference with, the local landscape should harm the wellbeing of themselves and their livestock. Similarly, families and whole lineages were totally preoccupied with the good or bad effects their ancestors' graves might bring. All were on the lookout for any signs that a good *fengshui* might have turned bad—as indicated by untoward events in the family, lineage, and village. Among numerous instances of *'fengshui* fixation', I have selected one from the past and another more recent.

The Shek Pik Valley
In the late 1950s, this valley on Lantau Island contained two main settlements, Shek Pik and Fan Pui. Their inhabitants were distributed among seven lineages settled there at different times over the previous 500 years. With ancestral halls, ancestral graves, genealogies, and, up to the 1920s, the traditional type of rural school with its teacher and classical textbooks, the villages had the strongly Confucian character typical of the region, though they appear not to have produced men with examination or even purchased degrees during the Qing dynasty.

The population of the villages began to fall from the mid nineteenth century onward. From a claimed peak population of nearly 1,000, only 363 people were recorded at the Hong Kong colony census of 1911, falling to around 260 forty years later. There had been no significant removals to other places, and few men had gone to work overseas. The dramatic reduction had been due to repeated epidemics of a disease, unidentified but recorded from elsewhere in the New

Territories, in which pig-like bristles and fish-like scales pushed out from the skin, and death could follow within several days.[2] Cattle, too, had sometimes died in large numbers: an outbreak of haemorrhagic septicaemia was recorded by government officials for Shek Pik and other places on Lantau in 1905. Lacking effective medical remedies and at the mercy of circumstances beyond their control, the villagers concluded that the local *fengshui* had changed for the worse and that the ancestors in their tombs had become malevolent towards the living.

We know little about the measures taken to deal with the general *fengshui* of the valley, but there is plenty of evidence to show what was done about the tombs. Several lineages consulted geomancers and moved their founding ancestors' graves to other locations, to calm them and restore good fortune to their descendants. Another dug up its first ancestor's grave and placed the burial urn separately, in another spot. In yet another, a geomancer had recommended retention of the old location, with adjustments to the orientation of the grave tablet.[3] According to the new tablet recording this change, the operation was completed on a lucky day in the tenth moon of 1886. No timing is given, but in a similar case noted in a New Territories' genealogy, for a grave built in 1840 and repaired in 1860, the adjustment itself had had to be made between 1 and 2 a.m. These major attempts at amelioration apart, regular visits to certain tombs at the grave worshipping festivals were discontinued.

It is highly significant that at some point the Shek Pik people had switched to a five- and later even to a two-and-a-half-yearly cycle for their *ta chiu* protective ritual, instead of following the ten-yearly cycle usual in the region; also that by the start of the twentieth century, the surviving members of three smaller lineages had, with consent, taken the names of larger ones. Some families had abandoned their ancestors altogether and went to the Roman Catholic mission in Tai O to become converts, and a few years later a Christian chapel was consecrated in an old village house donated by a widow.

Removal of all the inhabitants of the larger village to another site was the final step in this protracted and tense human drama. After decades of fruitless effort and expenditure of scarce cash, and prompted by yet another epidemic in the 1920s, most families abandoned their centuries-old homes in Shek Pik Wai and erected new houses on the rice-drying grounds a few hundred yards lower down the valley in what was thought to be a less dangerous location. Truly, the *fengshui* of the graves and of the old village had been regarded as 'a source of terror'.[4]

A generation later, when the consultant engineers to the Shek Pik Water Scheme began exploratory work in the valley in the mid 1950s, these events were things of the past, but they were still embedded in village minds and *fengshui* yet reigned supreme. The experience of engineers and officials put this beyond any doubt. However, the concern would now be more with the earth itself, rather than with the graves, because the site investigations were made in many places and involved clearing ground, exposing soil, drilling, and sampling. In an early incident of the kind, a Fan Pui villager hired by a contractor at the site refused to move stones from a path, and an attempt to blast a rock in the creek near one of the village temples brought on a full-scale confrontation. This was because local folklore linked the spot to an incident marking the onset of the bad *fengshui* narrated above. The exposure of the orange-red earth of localities within sight of habitations always led to agitation and representations.[5] This was also the case in all adjacent villages when land was required for the construction of access roads and catchwaters for the new reservoir. In one sensitive spot, the villagers would only permit the removal of rock by hand tools, and then only after the performance of *danfu* rituals and the placing of charms at selected locations (see Page 50).

Lung Yeuk Tau

Lung Yeuk Tau is an old village complex situated in the northern New Territories. It is one of the oldest and once most powerful settlements of the Deng lineage, which inhabits a number of similar village complexes there and in nearby Dongguan county. As in its other branches, there were many civil and military scholar-officials, both by examination and purchase, among its members during the Qing dynasty, Confucians all.

Like much of mainland New Territories, this area was affected by development in the mid 1980s. The villagers became alarmed at the impact on their landscape and its good *fengshui*, especially when their own plans to remedy the situation were rejected by the government. In their predicament, their leaders wrote to the District Officer, North to enlist his support, describing their situation in the following terms:

Our village has a history of some 800 years. Its *fengshui* is characterized by the windings of a phoenix river at its front and the backing of a dragon hill to its rear. Our main ancestral hall, temple, five walled settlements and six villages were built under the auspicious influences of the river and the hill. The five catalpa trees featuring the crouching dragon dominating the dragon hill, and the jade stream featuring the phoenix, together with the woodland along the banks of the river, have shielded us from harmful influences, enabling our [male] offspring to flourish and bringing peace and prosperity to the area for generations. But the landscape has been changed by site formation and the woodlands have been cut, owing to the government's development plans for the North District.

Moreover, its intention to erect pylons and electricity power lines across the dragon hill, thus severing it into two, has made all feel still more uneasy and upset.

The plan to restore the *fengshui* of the area derived from the advice of a geomancer who, after close examination of the whole area, confirmed the elders' fears in regard to the harm done by site excavation and tree-cutting. Central to the remedial process was the rebuilding of the very old Lung Kai Nunnery (Lung Shan Temple) to its former height and magnificence. Built on the lower slopes of the dragon hill, it had once (it was averred) possessed a nine-storey pagoda with powerful geomantic qualities. Only if it was rebuilt could the damage done to the *fengshui* of the dragon hill and phoenix river be offset. Moreover, the rebuilding would attract the protection of the gods.

The highly restrictive amendments to the plans required by the Buildings and Lands Department were reported along with the rest of the story. Only three storeys were permitted, and the planned enlargement of the temple had been turned down. However, without it, the *fengshui* of the area could not be restored, and as the leaders pointed out, their villagers 'would live in constant fear and would be deprived of peaceful and prosperous lives'.[6] The matter was reconsidered by the authorities, and ultimately, in 1993, the new temple was opened. In a compromise solution, it was larger than before and was seven storeys high (Plate 16).

Other Elements of the Belief System

Fengshui, and the steps taken to ensure or restore it, had little to do with Confucian teachings and mores. Neither did a number of other elements of village culture. Whereas Confucius had declined to speak on the subject, there was a universal belief in a wide range of powerful gods and spirits, to whom offerings could be made and prayers addressed, and in a myriad host of demons not well disposed towards humans, whose malevolence had to be deflected by one means or another. There was a strong disposition among village populations to attribute good or bad fortune to a very broad range of agencies, only matched by their eager willingness to believe in the efficacy of a wide variety of means to neutralize or correct them.

Recourse to the Gods

When epidemics had struck Shek Pik, no one had thought of praying to Confucius. Indeed, as we have seen, the ancestors were blamed for the disasters they were bringing on their descendants. At the last attack of disease in the 1920s, sick and weak, the headman had dragged himself to the village temple to supplicate its principal deity to save his family members from death and to make vows to obtain his help. And like him, most villagers had sought to enlist supernatural aid in these dire straits. It is significant that the temple was the only building left standing and maintained in Shek Pik Wai (Fig. 4.2).

It was the practice to apply to the gods for assistance in a wide variety of life's travails. Pleas for good fortune, safe journeys, recovery from sickness, and male children, to name only a few, were commonplace among individual requests. However, a temple's clientele (and income) depended on there being 'miracles'. Prayers had to be answered. As another missionary writer, Campbell M. Moody, observed in 1908, the Chinese people treated their recourse to temples like a

4.2 Hau Wong Temple at the abandoned site of Shek Pik Wai, the only building left standing and maintained in the old village, 1958. Named for a loyal Song-dynasty courtier who perished with his boy-emperor in battle in 1279, the temple encapsulates both Confucian virtues and non-Confucian beliefs.

shopping expedition. If one deity was deaf or ineffectual, best try another. The gods were also expected to help whole communities, as when plague threatened, when their portable images would be taken around a village, to the accompaniment of music and firecrackers, then placed in a specially erected matshed and worshipped by elders and people until the outbreak was over. Though no record remains, this practice was surely followed during the successive outbreaks of disease at Shek Pik.

The earth gods common to every village (and, being part of the official pantheon, to every government office) were equally regarded as protective spirits. Their shrines were an important focus for individual worship and for making requests, and as mentioned in Chapter 2, rituals were also performed there on behalf of the community. At Shek Pik, every day and all year round, oil and incense were offered at the earth god shrines in the village (Fig. 4.3) and at the earth god shrines below the altars in the two village temples. Village families took the first duty by rotation, whilst the duties in the temples were performed by the temple keepers, elderly local men appointed by the elders. However, the earth god shrines were few by comparison with the number of deities in any one locality. One village headman from Kwai Chung in the Tsuen Wan district stated that he had gone round his village area before its removal for development and had summoned 46 gods to take up residence in a general shrine at the resited village. The large number of local gods helps to explain why temporary altars were set up whenever a new house was to be built, and also why there was always an underlying concern whenever public works were begun in any locality (Plate 17).[7]

The Extensive Use of Charms

Like Confucianism, Daoism was a belief system native to China, but unlike the former, its philosophy had for long been overlaid with superstitious lore. It was once described by a missionary-scholar as being 'a diamond in a heap of rubbish'. By the nineteenth century, and long before, the

4.3 One of the abandoned *tudi gong* (earth god) shrines at Shek Pik Wai, worshipped at for the protection of village residents, 1958.

extensive worship of Daoist deities in the village temples, and the universal belief in spirits and demons, had been accompanied by an enormous production of Daoist charms designed to meet every conceivable human need. There existed a large body of priests and lay practitioners, villagers among them, who catered with their charms and rituals to human fears and travail, and managed rural crisis with their magic when the need arose. Protective and lucky charms were also available for placing on cow byres and pigsties, on agricultural implements, where they were practically universal, and even on the sluice gates allowing sea-water into enclosures used to trap marine creatures—all mostly done at the Lunar New Year.

Charms were much in use in time of sickness. Many temples possessed woodblock printed books of medical charms emanating from one or other of the various gods. Charms offering relief from all kinds of complaints and specific diseases can also be found in surviving manuscript handbooks formerly kept by villagers of the region (Fig. 4.4). All such charms were to be burned, and the ashes mixed with water or soup to be drunk by the patient. These charms could be found everywhere in China.[8] Charms of another sort were used to neutralize the ill effects of disturbed *fengshui*. These would be written by the priest or layman conducting the rituals, put in pots, and carried round the village in procession, accompanied by musicians. Placed one by one in strategic locations with the appropriate ritual prayers, the written charms would afford protection to the residents (Fig. 4.5). Known locally as *danfu*, the charms had to be renewed every six months for as long as the potential harm continued to threaten local people, in a *nuanfu* or 'warming' ritual.

When protection was sought in this way, it was usual to purchase new items connected with or used in the rituals,

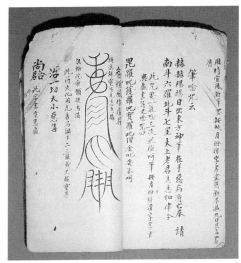

4.4 Medical charm for relieving headaches, from a village practitioner's handbook, a copy of which is to be burned and the ashes mixed with incense and drunk as a soup, Shek Pik *c.*1900.

4.5 Protective charms placed in a pot with incense near a grave on a hillside disturbed by a bulldozer, Tsing Yi, 1978.

and for those involved to purify themselves. When the Fan Pui villagers removed to their new homes in 1959, it was reported in a newspaper that 'they were in their new clothes with smiling faces'. Besides the firecrackers and religious ceremonies performed by Daoist priests and musicians on the removal day, they had washed their hair and bathed, and prior to the move had eaten only vegetarian food. Sexual abstinence was also prescribed.

Children were made aware of the existence of spirits and demons from an early age. Parents warned them to look out for the water spirit in this pond, the tree spirit in that grove of trees, and the like, perhaps, as one village friend has suggested, using them as 'bogeymen' in an effort to keep their children out of mischief or danger. Keeping infants and young children safe was a major preoccupation. They were given the very common protective silver lockets to wear, and many parents engaged Daoist priests to carry out rituals of adoption before tree spirits or temple deities, in order to enlist their aid during the dangerous period before a child becomes an adult, as recorded in one of the Shek Pik genealogies. Similar ceremonies of 'release' were performed at the end of this period, when thanks were rendered for safekeeping.

Evil spirits could also be kept away by putting up old copies of the Almanac. The sections printed in red were deemed especially effective, a supposition supported by the Cantonese saying that demons fear the red ink used for writing charms. You could also get a charm to write on the palm of your hand to protect you from demons when you went out in the dark. In another common procedure, Daoist practitioners advised on which people should stay away from various rituals, including weddings and funerals, depending upon the year of their birth and the related animal of the Chinese zodiac, and could also indicate the places where a bridal chair should be set down upon entering the bridegroom's house.

Buddhist Elements

Buddhism, too, provided services to the common people. Its priests could perform some of the protective rituals performed by Daoists, but were more specifically associated with the many rites connected with death and the hoped-for safe passage of the soul through the underworld. Buddhism itself was a powerful force among women, whose lives were often liable to be bitter, fraught with the danger and sorrows of childbirth and rearing children. For one missionary writer, Buddhism brought heaven and earth near to one another for the mass of the people. In the practice of prayer, and in the conception of the afterlife, it was, he wrote, 'bridging the gulf which Confucius leaves almost unbridgeable', owing to the sage's lack of attention to the hereafter and the spirit world.

A Harmonious Interweaving

Thus the basic Confucianism visible in village life had long been accompanied by an equally massive accretion of non-Confucian elements. This was to be expected, for Confucianism was an austere creed and did not meet all human needs, particularly those arising from fear and sorrow. Yet in another of their applications, Daoist and Buddhist beliefs and practices reinforced the moral values of Confucianism by threatening offenders with dire punishment in the hereafter. Thus the so-called Three Religions existed together in a quasi-unitary and complementary mode. No southern Chinese villager could dispense with any one of them.

Notes

1   See Evelyn Lip (1987) for a photograph of the geomancer's compass. Much of the information in this paragraph is taken from her book.

2   This disease appears to be within the trichothiodystrophic spectrum of diseases, in which scaling of the skin, brittle hair and nails, and sudden hair loss when the temperature exceeds 41°C, all occur during high fever. See Vermeulen, W., et. al. in *Nature Genetics*, vol. 27, pp. 299–303, 2001. I am indebted to my friend Ian Dunn for this reference.

3   Similarly, the doors of houses and ancestral halls could be slanted away from the direction of the parent building to assure better *fengshui*, adjustments considered necessary because of concern over lack of male births. The height of the altar on which the ancestral tablets stood within a hall might also be adjusted, to ensure a better line of sight to the local *fengshui*.

4   Several other Lantau villages took similar action to restore their *fengshui* about that time, after population losses and lack of male births. The Deng lineage also regarded this particular cycle as having brought troubles to its village communities. Though in no way detracting from the extraordinary trauma experienced by the Shek Pik population, there is a general background of heavy mortality in traditional village life to add to this account. On the basis of his analysis of the two Hong Kong census reports of 1911 and 1922, Dr Patrick Hase (1996) has concluded that 'of all live births, one quarter were dead by about age 7–8, half by 22–24, and three-quarters by the age of 48 (females), or 54 (men)'.

5   More detail is given in Chapter Two of my book, *Friends and Teachers*: 1996.

6   Dr Patrick Hase, who has considerable expertise in this field, very kindly examined the area at my request. He confirms that the temple site is of very great importance to the *fengshui* of Lung Yeuk Tau and warranted its reconstruction, but queries whether a nine-storey structure was required. He also questions the degree of harm from site formation for development. On the other hand, the power lines have weakened the *fengshui* of the area. I am grateful to him for determining the geomantic position and taking photographs.

7   Dr Carole Morgan (1996) has reminded us recently that disturbance of the ground—in this case related to digging tombs, but of general relevance—has long excited concern among the Chinese, traceable to the cult of the Earth and its divine personification, Houtu, mentioned in the *Zuozhuan*, a work compiled in the third century BC.

8   Nearly 100 years ago, Henri Doré collected a great many charms in Central China, and published the famous series noted in the Bibliography. Doré's work is still an indispensable guide to the notions prevailing in the contemporary village world.

5
Women and Girls in Traditional Village Culture

Goods on which one loses one's capital
—traditional Chinese saying about girls

Male Superiority, Female Subjugation

IN KEEPING WITH the extent to which Confucianism had come to dominate village culture, it is hardly surprising to find that rural society was characterized by male dominance and female subordination. The phrase still in common use, 'China is a nation that lays emphasis on males and discounts females', was nothing less than a fact. In their elder years, it is true, paternal grandmothers were accorded much respect by their sons' families, but otherwise women generally fared badly. There are various pointers as to how village men regarded the opposite sex.

The terminology of marriage is instructive. In the arranged marriages that were the rule, when a man married off his son, his family 'took a daughter-in-law'. When a father agreed to the terms of his daughter's marriage, she was described in local village terms as 'being sold off'. This was because a bride price (that is, the sum to be paid to the bride's parents upon settlement of a marriage) was negotiated between the parties by a go-between. The down-to-earth nature of these transactions at the village level is made clear by the answers given by elderly villagers to questions on the subject. Mulling over the going rate for a bride price in his youth, the Shek Pik headman compared it to the cost of buying a pig, or to the sum paid for one of the small rice fields in the valley.

Two types of marriage were possible for a girl. She could have a 'big' marriage, with a betrothal (often entered into for her when young or in infancy) and bride price, or she could have a 'small' marriage. The latter was much less esteemed, since it meant that she had gone to another family when very young to be a *san po tsai* or 'little daughter-in-law', as the future wife of one of its sons. Neither bride price nor dowry were required, and the customary banquet for the village and lineage was optional. Marriages of this sort usually took place among poor families, and were determined by poverty or sudden misfortune in the girl's family, such as the death of a parent.

In the same way, there was little ceremony for a woman or girl going to 'fill the room' (as the term *tin fong* translates) of a deceased wife. There was even less fuss when a young widow was remarried, reflecting the Confucian view that remarriage for women was to be deprecated: rather she should honour her late husband's memory by remaining single and alone. A widow might also have to rear a son found for her by the elders so that ancestral sacrifices to her late husband might be performed. As a matter of course, women and girls were excluded from the Confucian rites in the hall of ancestors or at the grave, and could not share, in their own right, in the sacrificial pork usually distributed on these occasions.

Another glimpse of the status of women is provided by the entries in the handwritten genealogies possessed by many village lineages. The married women of the lineage are usually recorded by their own family names, without mention of their personal names or home villages. A man's daughters are listed by number, and seldom by name. Female graves are noted mostly in cases where a wife's remains have been placed in a formal grave with her husband's. Here, as model Confucian wives, respect and even eulogy might, at last, be granted to them on the grave tablets.

56

Perhaps the most telling evidence for the depressed female status is that whereas boys were often adopted from within the lineage to provide male heirs, and seldom sold, there was much trafficking in female children and young girls. Female missionaries to China recorded many sad cases of the kind in the course of their work among women and girls, in town and country alike. In this light it is scarcely surprising that Herbert Giles, former British Consul and leading authority on China, could write: 'It is perhaps superfluous to state that . . . a girl is really, even at a very early age, a marketable commodity.' Taken all in all, the foregoing account adds weight to what my late mother-in-law (born near Canton in 1907) used to say: 'Women had to exercise a lot of patience in the old society, putting up with many things they did not like but could not change.' It was, she added, even worse in the countryside.

Lack of Education

Girls were seldom educated. An elderly villager once described the situation in the following terms: 'Whereas nowadays men and women are equal, previously women were expected to stay at home, minding the children and looking after the household. People deemed it unnecessary to educate girls, considering it a waste of money, especially as they would marry out of the family and any benefit would go to the husband's folk. That's the way they thought in the old days.' His assessment is amply borne out by the results of Hong Kong census-taking. At the 1911 colony census, only 466 women in the New Territories were recorded as being literate, compared with 33,424 who were not.

Besides being unable to read or write, women in many places led isolated lives. The 86-year-old Shek Pik lady, pictured leaving her village to travel to her new home in Tsuen Wan in 1960 (Plate 18), was like many of her kind. Born on Lantau Island, she had never left it during her long life, nor had she actually seen a car or lorry until site investigations began on the large reservoir whose construction led to the removal of all the villagers, herself included.

Poor Quality of Female Life

The quality of women's lives would depend to a large degree on the class of society into which they were born and married. It would be higher in wealthy families and lower in poorer ones, especially in the villages, where besides their work in preparing food (Fig. 5.1), the women and girls were required to do a good deal of the heavy work of the farm.

In many areas, with menfolk overseas or away from home, there was no option. The New Territories Evangelization Society's report for 1915 bewailed the fact that, 'Over considerable areas the women and girls do, practically, all the field work, heavy and light, including the plowing of the soil.' Clad in rough hemp garments, they had to plough and harrow fields with oxen or brown cattle (Fig. 5.2). Even where male relatives were present, it was often common practice for men and women to work the land together.

Another major task for village women, come rain or shine, was to cut and carry grass and firewood from the hillsides (Fig. 5.3). Seen from a distance, a European hiker once described the women as 'miniature haystacks wandering on the mountainside'. The commodities were used at home in cooking meals and preparing pig food, and large bundles of

5.1 Hakka women grinding soy beans in a street outside Kowloon Walled City, *c.*1950 (courtesy of the Hong Kong Museum of History).

5.2 Woman ploughing with an ox through heavy clay-rich earth, probably northern New Territories, *c.*1930 (courtesy of the Hong Kong Museum of History).

the grass and firewood were also carried many miles to the market towns to sell. Older women could achieve a measure of relief from these heavy duties only when their sons married. In response to a rather naive question about when she had stopped going up to the hills, one old lady gave me the tart response, 'When I got a daughter-in-law!'

Other occupations were less strenuous, and included tending hemp and indigo plants, and preparing dyestuffs and hemp threads for sewing and weaving. Sewing embroideries with auspicious designs and weaving were also common tasks in the home: the distinctive, coloured patterned bands, worn by Hakka women as straps for headgear and aprons (Plate 19), were among the items woven, and it was the custom for girls to give them to female relatives at the time

5.3 A cheerful village woman carrying grass cut from the hillside, c.1951 (courtesy of Tim Ko).

of their marriage. Many women acquired or inherited a knowledge of simples, and could be seen collecting the necessary medicinal herbs from the hillsides for home use, or taking them to sell on the streets of the market towns. A few developed skills as midwives or shamans, or in weaving hats and baskets with the rattan found in the hills around the villages.

Suicides but a General Robustness

Suicides among young women were not uncommon, as a young wife's lot could sometimes prove beyond endurance. A District Officer's annual report of 1938 mentions their prevalence, and named the poisonous plants commonly used in such cases. The causes of self-destruction were varied, and could include a demanding or tyrannical mother-in-law (it was both by tradition and practice for them to be such), endless work from dawn till dusk, the prospect of childbirth under primitive and highly adverse conditions, and endemic malaria or similar diseases. A countryside jingle from Lantau Island, derived from the call of the koel in spring, is a reminder of how bad things could be for a young wife. Taken to represent the words *ka-kung ka-po, tak-tsui lo-po* (father-in-law, mother-in-law, making daughter-in-law unhappy), it was linked to the legend of the suicide of a young woman with a harridan for a mother-in-law.[1]

Yet young women were mostly robust in their approach to the customs of the times. Many female informants had gone in procession to upland villages by bridal chair, to join husbands and families they had never seen. Their marriages had been arranged through a go-between, usually a woman who knew the circumstances of both families. Each family preferred to employ a person known to them, sometimes a relative or someone coming from their own village, as providing for greater security and peace of mind in such important family business. Those who became 'little daughters-in-law' had their special trials through having to grow up in their future husbands' families. Some experienced rough, even harsh, treatment at their hands, but this was often recalled with wry amusement by some women, among them the 76-year-old lady shown in Plate 20, encountered on a visit to Pingshan in the Hakka area of Shenzhen in 1990, who was among the more cheerful sort. Her husband-to-be was one of three brothers, and two years her senior when she was sent to his home at the age of four. All three brothers had *san po tsai* brought into the family, and there were over ten people in the household.

Fun and Festivities

Yet village life was not all misery and drabness for women. The main festivals of the lunar year brought colour and activity to most households, since every attempt was made to make them special and enjoyable. The emphasis was on eating, and special foods were made at home to mark the particular season. The other feature of the major holiday of the year, the extended period during Lunar New Year, was leisure for talk and entertainment, including singing and games of chance played with other females.

Until their children had grown up, and parents, aunts, and uncles had died off, it was common for young married women to take their offspring to visit their home village at one or other of the main festival times. Old men recall going along with their mothers on these visits, when parties of gaily chattering women would set off across the hills on the journey there and back, creating a happy atmosphere for those encountering them en route. Another form of enjoyment was provided by the *shan ko* or mountain songs, which were sung at a distance between women and girl grass-cutters of different villages, sometimes with men, and also between children of either sex tending cows in the hills. Since improvisation featured in these song exchanges, they could also represent rare moments of self-expression.

Women as Teachers and Role Models

Naturally, as mothers and grandmothers, women played an important role in bringing up children. As mentioned in Chapter 3, this included teaching them the courtesies that were part of the Confucian system. Though mostly illiterate themselves, they sought to instil the correct terms of address for family relationships on the male and female sides of the family, and to see that the children greeted relatives appropriately. They would also instruct the boys how to perform worship at the tombs; to kneel behind the feast laid out in front of the graves, move their fully extended arms up and down in token of respect to their forebears, and intone the prayers made on such occasions.

In their daily lives, serving their parents-in-law, rearing children, instructing the young, and performing their multifarious household and farm duties, women, like the men, had paragons held up for their attention. Famous women like Mencius' mother, and others in the catalogue of Chinese female virtue, provided role models for them to emulate. Sometimes the mandarins singled out virtuous women for praise. On a hill near one of the Tsuen Wan

5.4 The spirit tablet of the Virtuous Woman (*c.*1870).

5.5 Virtuous Woman's Memorial Temple, Tsing Lung Tau, Tsuen Wan.

villages is the grave of a married woman who committed suicide after being kidnapped and placed in a brothel. The officers of the nearby customs post on Ma Wan rescued her body from the sea and prepared a formal grave, whilst the district magistrate invited a scholar to compose a eulogy for her commemorative tablet. She also has a special shrine in the nearby temple complex (Figs. 5.4 and 5.5).

Religiosity of Women

Many women found solace in religion. The greater fervour and attendance of women in the temples and other religious houses was remarked on by Christian missionaries. The biographer of Revd Robert Morrison, the first Protestant missionary to China, wrote in 1889 that 'their nature is much more religious than that of the men. The men trifle with their beliefs; the women are in earnest. ...It is they who visit the temples. ...They burn ten sheets of paper to the men's one. ...When the men pretend to worship them [the images of various deities] they only play at it. ...They make much better Christians than the men.' Another missionary affirmed the general experience, that 'women form the stronghold of the faith'.

Female religiosity is still much in evidence today in Hong Kong's favoured city and rural temples, and religious houses. It is especially evident during each of the four 'birthdays' celebrated for Guan Yin, the Goddess of Mercy, a deity particularly favoured by women (Plate 21). The couplets adorning the main worshipping halls emphasize the compassionate nature of Buddhism, bringing solace to grieving or anxious women, and hope of future relief to those presently enjoying good health and fortune. Another deity specially favoured by women, past and present, is the Daoist Lady Kam Fa or Golden Flower, whose image can be found on side altars in many temples in the region.

A Retrospect

Viewed overall, women's contribution to village culture was complementary to men's. Despite their subordinate status and its concomitants—the lack of education, and an exceedingly hard and difficult life—the sterling qualities often to be found among the adult females of rural families strengthened their lineages and communities. The women were usually endowed with fortitude and strength of character, backed by a simple but sincere faith, whilst their high degree of conservatism did much to sustain village life and culture over many centuries.

Notes

1 Putting words to bird calls in order to perpetuate old legends is recorded elsewhere. For two examples from Zhejiang province, see Venerable Arthur Evans Moule, *Half a Century in China* (London: Hodder and Stoughton, *c.*1911), pp. 147–8. There is another charming instance in Colin Campbell Brown's *Children of China* (Edinburgh: Oliphant, Anderson and Ferrier, 1909), pp. 48–9.

6

Heritage Awareness and Preservation

*[Preservation] of the local heritage...helps to make history
into a valuable living experience*
—S. M. Bard, 1988

THIS IS NOT the place to enter into details of how change has affected the rural communities of Hong Kong and Shenzhen in the last half century. There has been continuous development and redevelopment in Hong Kong, whilst across the former Sino–British border the austere thirty years of Maoist revolution were followed by Deng Xiaoping's Four Modernizations policies and the establishment of the Shenzhen Special Economic Zone. In both places an ever-extending high-rise urbanization has been pushing rural life to one side, where it has not extinguished it altogether. Yet despite the continuing emphasis being laid on change and modernity everywhere in the region today, the legacy of the past is not being ignored either. Hong Kong and Shenzhen can each point to achievements in this field, with the major initiatives in preservation, conservation, and the collection of artefacts of the material culture all coming from government institutions.

Hong Kong

In Hong Kong, an Antiquities Advisory Board, and an Antiquities and Monuments Office to service its work, were established in the mid 1970s, to give effect to an ordinance enacted in 1973. Their work has been done with public and private funds, including finance from corporate donors, and more recently by the Lord Wilson Heritage Trust, and in some cases has been facilitated by the cooperation of far-sighted village owners. There are now many restored old buildings of historical importance and architectural merit (Plates 22 and 23). Some historic forts and batteries have also been restored. Attention is being paid to groups of structures, and with local consent, heritage trails have been designated in two of the oldest and largest New Territories' villages, enabling the visitor to enjoy historic buildings within their authentic social milieu. There were 70 declared monuments on 18 August 2000, whilst 452 other historical buildings and structures, as well as archaeological sites, had been recorded and graded.[1]

Shenzhen

In Shenzhen, the walled city of Nantou, its most important single historical entity, has been the subject of considerable expenditure since the 1980s. Its surviving walled gateways and overhead guardhouses have been restored (Plate 24), and inside the city several of the official buildings and temples have been rebuilt to their original style. Commemorative plaques have been positioned, and full-sized replicas of certain inscribed imperial tablets that stood within the walls have been erected. Outside the South Gate, the text on a large information board refers to the reunification of Hong Kong and Macau with China, and explains that the purpose of the renovation programmes in the walled city is to 'purify the people's hearts'.[2]

Not far from Nantou, the famous Tianhou Temple at Chiwan has been rebuilt. Its long history and cultural importance had not saved it from destruction during the Cultural Revolution (1966–1976). Only the foundations remained. One feature of the restoration project is worth noting: in Shenzhen, as elsewhere in the adjoining districts during the reconstruction of historic and popular temples, the opportunity is being taken to build on a larger scale than the original, but in the now favoured Beijing Palace–style, rather than in the regional vernacular. In this particular case, the result has been to make the Tianhou Temple look quite different from its earlier appearance over the past 600 years (Plate 25).[3]

Museum Collections

In Hong Kong, the two former municipal museums, established in 1962 and 1986, occupy new, custom-built premises in Kowloon and Sha Tin. They are now called the Hong Kong Museum of History and the Hong Kong Heritage Museum, respectively. Their staff have collected many artefacts from village culture of the past, and have also provided permanent exhibitions on local history and ethnography in their main and branch premises. An energetic campaign mounted by the former Regional Council and its museum in 1995 secured over 6,000 objects by public donation, mostly from the village communities of the New Territories with the enthusiastic help of many local leaders. The two museums provide educational and outreach programmes, and their activities complement the preservation of older buildings, as well as the work of the Antiquities and Monuments Office.

The Shenzhen Museum opened in 1988, relatively early in the development of the zone. Its staff have carried out many surveys at archaeological and historical sites, and as in Hong Kong have built up collections and arranged public displays illustrating the history and prehistory of the area, besides providing extensive information in separate rooms about the modern industries and amenities of the Special Economic Zone. Publication is also a feature of the museum's work. Meantime, at the time of writing a new museum is under construction. Other smaller collections are being assembled in historic centres within the municipality.

Preservation of Written Materials

The village culture of the Hong Kong region relied heavily on written materials for carrying on the business of everyday life and for the transmission of culture and local traditions (see Chapter 3). The recovery and conservation of these fragile items from the cultural repertoire is just as essential as preserving buildings and durable objects from everyday life. A wide range of printed and manuscript materials was collected in the villages by student teams from the Chinese University of Hong Kong from the late 1970s on, working under the direction of David Faure and others. In addition, in 1986 the former Urban Council published three volumes of historical inscriptions from Hong Kong, with major assistance from Dr Faure. The private libraries of several village scholars have also been preserved. All such material is kept in specialized university and public libraries.[4]

In Shenzhen, the position may be less favourable, owing to the likely destruction of many documents during land reform and the sustained ideological fervour of the years of Mao Zedong (1949–1976). Nonetheless, the Shenzhen Museum has a collection of land deeds, along with family

70

and business papers, similar in type to the materials collected in Hong Kong.

Supporting Studies

A good deal of intensive, detailed research is being undertaken by the universities of Hong Kong and Guangdong province into many aspects of traditional culture. These studies complement the restoration and conservation being implemented by other agencies, and assist public awareness and understanding. Moreover, through beginning at the bottom, in the towns and villages where most people lived, this new scholarly effort is part of the current movement seeking to understand Chinese culture as a whole, through what Daniel L. Overmyer has styled its 'demographic foundations', rather than (as in the past) by viewing it from the top down.[5]

In Conclusion

This short account of the work being done to preserve and conserve the material and documentary evidence of traditional village culture concludes the overview attempted in this book. Those concerned seem to share the outlook of the Republican scholar Carson Chang who, back in 1958, advised us most earnestly not to write off the past. 'China', he wrote, 'happens to be animated by a living consciousness of the most impressive historical continuity', and is 'an organism and not a museum'. Hence accounts such as that attempted in these pages are not the antiquarian exercise they may seem. Also, the 'Chineseness' of China was essentially rooted in the villages, as true for Guangdong province as elsewhere. Despite sweeping material, social, and political change, essential elements of the old culture remain, evinced in behavioural patterns that embody the various component elements described in this book.

Notes

1   Publication has accompanied conservation. The Antiquities Advisory Board issues periodic reports on its work, and the Antiquities and Monuments Office has produced a series of brochures on historic buildings and other antiquities.

2   The text of this notice is reminiscent of the admonitory tablets from the reigns of two emperors of the Qing dynasty—Yongzheng (r.1723–1736) and Qianlong (r.1736–1796). Erected inside the city, they listed what the emperors styled the 'four evils and obnoxious things' (including gambling, opium-smoking, and prostitution), and urged their subjects to improve their conduct. One of the originals remains.

3   The work in Nantou Old City and at the Tianhou Temple at Chiwan has been largely the work of one man. Mr Zhang Yibeng acted on behalf of the several local authorities, but as and where possible undertook private fund-raising. Many people and organizations from Hong Kong and Dongguan county helped restore the Tianhou Temple, and their names and contributions are listed on commemorative tablets on site.

4   As well as in Hong Kong, materials relating to the region are also being kept in major overseas collections. Many land documents and miscellaneous papers are preserved in the East Asian Collection at the Hoover Institution of Stanford University, and a major collection of genealogies from Hong Kong and Guangdong province is kept by the Genealogical Society of Utah, The Church of Jesus Christ of Latter-day Saints in Salt Lake City.

5   Daniel L. Overmyer, 'On the foundations of Chinese culture in late traditional times...', in Daniel L. Overmyer and Shin-Yi Chao (eds.), *Ethnography in China Today: A Critical Assessment of Methods and Results* (Taiwan: Yuan-liou Publication Company, expected in 2002). This article is a review of volumes 1 and 5, edited by Fang Xuejia, in the Traditional Hakka Society Series (series editor John Lagerwey), published by the International Hakka Studies Association and the École Française d'Extrême-Orient in 1996 and 1997.

Glossary

WHILE EVERY EFFORT has been made to include entries in the Glossary in alphabetical order, different romanizations make it difficult to provide a uniform presentation. Where possible, the Cantonese romanization is given first in alphabetical order; all pinyin romanizations appear in parentheses.

(Baoan)	寶安縣	County absorbed into Shenzhen municipality in 1993.
(*biane*)	匾額	'Honorary tablets consist of names of buildings, brief congratulatory statements, pleas for spiritual blessings, or records of examination successes, mostly on horizontal wooden boards' (David Faure).
Chan Tak-hang	陳德亨	A member of the rural gentry.
Chek Wan (Chiwan)	赤灣	Locality near Nantou.
Chow-Wong (Zhou-Wang)	周王 (周有德王來任)	Memorial temples to these two officials, under various names.
chi tong (*ci tang*)	祠堂	Hall of ancestors, ancestral hall.
(*dibao*)	地保	Rural agent.
(*di shi*)	地師	Expert in land (geomancer).
(*di xue*)	地學	Land learning (*fengshui*).
fai chun	揮春	Lunar New Year couplets to welcome the spring.
Fuk Wing (Fuyong)	福永	Locality in Shenzhen.
fung shui (fengshui)	風水	Geomancy.
fung shui sin sang (*fengshui xiansang*)	風水先生	A geomancer.
ga chong (*jia zhang*)	嫁妝	Dowry.
(Guoyuanshiju)	果園世居	A village in Shenzhen.

(Gushu)	固戍	A village in Shenzhen.
Hau Wong (Houwang)	侯王	Deity of the Shek Pik Wai village temple.
(He Zhen)	何真(東莞伯)	Earl of Dongguan.
Honam (Henan)	河南	Island opposite Canton.
(Houtu)	后土	Divine personification of Earth.
(Huidong)	惠東縣	A county to the east of Shenzhen municipality.
Hung Shing (Hongsheng)	洪聖	Popular deity in South China.
(Jiulongshan)	九龍山	Locality in Huidong.
kaifong	街坊	Management committee in a town or market town.
ka-kung ka-po tak-tsui lo-po	家公家婆得罪老婆	Country jingle.
Kam Fa (Jinhua)	金花夫人	Lady Kam Fa; popular deity with women in South China.
Kan Ting Shu Shat (Guanting shushi)	觀廷書室	Study hall in the New Territories.
(*kejiaban*)	科甲班	Persons achieving a degree or appointment by public examination; the 'regular' entry route to the Qing bureaucracy.
(*juanban*)	捐班	Persons purchasing a degree or appointment, the 'irregular' entry route to the Qing bureaucracy throughout the dynasty, especially in its cash-strapped later years of rebellion, natural disasters, and wars with foreign powers.
lai kam (*lijin*)	禮金	Bride price, marriage settlement in cash.
law pun (*luopan*)	羅盤	Geomancer's compass.

Lit Ching Chi (Liezhenci)	烈貞祠	Virtuous Woman's Memorial Temple, Tsing Lung Tau, Tsuen Wan.
Liu Man Shek Tong (Liao Wanshitang)	廖萬石堂	The main ancestral hall in Sheung Shui village.
Lung Kai Nunnery	龍溪庵	Now rebuilt and renamed Lung Shan Temple, Lung Yeuk Tau, northern New Territories.
Lungtianshiju	龍田世居	A walled village in Shenzhen.
Man (Wen)	文	A large lineage/clan in Xinan county.
(Mao)	毛	A lineage settled in the New Territories.
Mencius (Mengzi)	孟子	Chinese philosopher *c.*371–*c.*289 BC noted for developing Confucianism.
Nam Tau (Nantou)	南頭	County seat of Xinan.
nuen fu (*nuanfu*)	暖符	'Warming' ritual, renewing protection.
(Pingshan)	平山	Locality in Shenzhen.
sai chui (*xiaoqu*)	細娶	'Small' marriage, without bride price, dowry, bridal chair, or procession.
Sai Chuk Lam	西竺林	Religious house above Tsuen Wan, New Territories.
Sai Heung (Xixiang)	西鄉	Locality in Shenzhen.
san chu pai (*shenzhupai*)	神主牌	Ancestor tablet.
San On (Xinan)	新安縣	New Peace county.
san po tsai	新抱仔	Little daughter-in-law.
Sham Chun (Shenzhen)	深圳	The Shenzhen municipality, and the former market town of Shenzhen.

shan ko	山歌	Mountain songs.
Sheung Yue Tung	雙魚洞	Double Fish Division.
(Sungang)	笋崗圍	A village in Shenzhen.
ta chiu (tajiao)	打醮	A protective ritual for old communities, performed with the aid of Daoist priests every ten years or less, accompanied by opera or puppet plays for the deities.
tai chui (daqu)	大娶	'Big' (adult) marriage with bride price, dowry, bridal chair and procession, and banquet.
Tang (Deng)	鄧	A large lineage in Xinan and adjacent counties.
tin fong (tianfang)	填房	'Filling the room' of a deceased wife.
Tin Hau (Tianhou)	天后	The Queen of Heaven, a popular deity in South China.
tong yan	唐人	'Men of Tang', the term used by Cantonese people to describe themselves, as differentiating from the northern 'Men of Han'.
to tei kung (tudi gong)	土地公	Earth gods.
tso, or *tong (zu*, or *tang)*	祖堂	Land- or property-owning lineage trusts; different institutions but with some shared aims.
Tsui (Xu)	徐	One of the lineages in Shek Pik village.
tun fu (danfu)	蛋符	Written charms used in a protective ritual.
(Wen Tianxiang)	文天祥	Song-dynasty statesman, poet, and patriot (1236–1283).
yeuk (yue)	約	Alliances between groups of villages, creating local sub-divisions of the county.

(Zhang Yibeng)	張一平	Chiefly responsible for the restoration work in Shenzhen.
(Zhu Xi)	朱熹	Neo-Confucian philosopher (1130–1200) whose reshaping of Confucian doctrine and practice endured until the end of the Qing dynasty.

The Chinese Classics

The core works of the Confucian Canon are summarized in the Appendix to Thompson, 1969. They include the *Four Books* and *Five Classics*, together comprising the *Great Learning, Doctrine of the Mean, Analects,* and *Works of Mencius*: the *Book of Changes, Book of Odes, Book of History, Canon of Rites,* and *Spring and Autumn Annals*. This latter includes a book known as *Zuo's Commentary* (*Zuozhuan*) (see Page 54 n. 7). The *Book of Odes* is also known as the *Book of Poetry*.

The *Trimetric Classic* is an elementary school primer of the Southern Song period (1127–1279), 'which is still the primer committed to memory by every Chinese lad' (W. F. Mayers, 1876).

Another primer, the '*Ti tzu kuei or Rules of Behaviour for Children*', is stated by Isaac Taylor Headland (*The Young China Seekers*: 1912, translation pp. 66–76) to be 'the foundation of all Chinese etiquette, as the *San tzu ching* [*Trimetric Classic*] is the foundation of their general education. ...It is largely used in Chinese schools and studied by the children of the better classes.'

Selected Bibliography

By DEFINITION, this list cannot provide references for all the quotations which appear in the text. The aim is to indicate works that have been most useful to the author and will be helpful to readers wishing to know more.

Baker, Hugh D. R., *Sheung Shui, A Chinese Lineage Village*, London: Frank Cass, 1968.

———, *Ancestral Images; More Ancestral Images;* and *Ancestral Images Again*, Hong Kong: South China Morning Post Ltd, 1979, 1980, and 1981, respectively.

Ball, J. Dyer, *The Pith of the Classics: The Chinese Classics in Everyday Life*, Hong Kong: Noronha and Co., 1905.

Bard, Solomon, *In Search of the Past, A Guide to Hong Kong's Antiquities*, Hong Kong: Urban Council, 1988.

Doré, Henri, SJ, *Chinese Customs*, Singapore: Graham Brash, 1987. This is a facsimile of the English translation of the first volume of Doré's great work by M. Kennelly, SJ, *Researches into Chinese Superstitions*, 13 vols., Shanghai: T'usewei Press, 1914.

Eastman, Lloyd E., *Family, Fields, and Ancestors: Constancy and Change in China's Social and Economic History, 1550–1949*, New York: Oxford University Press, 1988.

Ebrey, Patricia, 'The Chinese Family and the Spread of Confucian Values' in Gilbert Rozman (ed.), *The East Asian Region, Confucian Heritage and its Modern Adaptation*, Princeton: Princeton University Press, 1991, pp. 45–83.

Faure, David, *The Structure of Chinese Rural Society, Lineage and Village in the Eastern New Territories of Hong Kong*, Hong Kong: Oxford University Press, 1986.

Freedman, Maurice, *Chinese Lineage and Society, Fukien and Kwangtung*, London: University of London, The Athlone Press, 1966.

Garrett, Valery M., *Chinese Clothing: An Illustrated Guide*, Hong Kong: Oxford University Press, 1994.

Hase, Patrick, 'New Territories Poetry and Song' in *Collected Essays on Various Historical Materials for Hong Kong Studies* (bilingual), Hong Kong: Hong Kong Museum of History for Urban Council, 1990, pp. 20–32 (illustrated).

———, 'Traditional Life in the New Territories: The Evidence of the 1911 and 1922 Censuses', *Journal of the Hong Kong Branch of the Royal Asiatic Society*, vol. 36, 1996, pp. 1–92.

Hase, Patrick H., and Lee Man-yip, 'Sheung Wo Hang Village, Hong Kong: A Village Shaped by Fengshui' in Ronald G. Knapp (ed.), *Chinese Landscapes: The Village as Place*, Honululu: University of Hawaii Press, 1992, pp. 79–94.

Hase, Patrick. H., and Sinn, Elizabeth (eds.), *Beyond the Metropolis: Villages in Hong Kong*, Hong Kong: Royal Asiatic Society, Hong Kong branch, with Joint Publishing (HK) Ltd., 1995.

Hayes, James, *The Hong Kong Region 1850–1911: Institutions and Leadership in Town and Countryside*, Hamden, Conn.: Archon Books, 1977.

———, *The Rural Communities of Hong Kong: Studies and Themes*, Hong Kong: Oxford University Press, 1983.

———, 'Specialists and Written Materials in the Village World', in David Johnson, Andrew J. Nathan, and Evelyn S. Rawski (eds.), *Popular Culture in Late Imperial China*, Berkeley: University of California Press, 1987, pp. 75–111.

———, *Friends and Teachers: Hong Kong and Its People 1953–87*, Hong Kong: Hong Kong University Press, 1996.

Hummel, Arthur, W., Foreword to Atwood, Elaine Spaulding's translation with annotation and illustrations of Chavannes, Edouard, *The Five Happinesses, Symbolism in Chinese*

Popular Art [first published in French in 1901], New York: Weatherhill, 1973.

Johnson, Elizabeth, *Recording a Rich Heritage: Research on Hong Kong's 'New Territories'*, Hong Kong: Leisure and Cultural Services Department, Hong Kong SAR Government, 2000.

Knapp, Ronald G., *China's Living Houses: Folk Beliefs, Symbols, and Household Ornamentation*, Honolulu: University of Hawaii Press, 1999.

———, *China's Old Dwellings*, Honolulu: University of Hawaii Press, 2000.

Krone, Revd Mr, 'A Notice of the Sanon District', *Transactions of the China Branch, Royal Asiatic Society*, 6 (1859), pp. 71–105. Reprinted in the *Journal of the Hong Kong Branch of the Royal Asiatic Society*, 7 (1967), pp. 104–137.

Law, Joan and Ward, Barbara E., *Chinese Festivals in Hong Kong*, Hong Kong: South China Morning Post, 1982.

Lim, Patricia, *Discovering Hong Kong's Cultural Heritage*, Hong Kong: Oxford University Press, 1997.

Lip, Evelyn, *Feng Shui, A Layman's Guide to Chinese Geomancy*, Union City, CA: Heian International, Inc., 1987.

Lung, David Y. P., *Chinese Traditional Vernacular Architecture*, Hong Kong: Regional Council, 1991.

Morgan, Carole, 'Traces of Houtu's Cult in Hong Kong', *Journal of the Hong Kong Branch of the Royal Asiatic Society*, vol. 36, 1996, pp. 223–225.

Mote, F. W., *Imperial China 900–1800*, Cambridge, Massachusetts, and London, England: Harvard University Press, 1999.

Needham, Joseph, *Within the Four Seas: The Dialogue of East and West*, London: George Allen & Unwin, 1969.

Ng, Peter Y. L., and Baker, Hugh, *New Peace County: A Chinese Gazetteer of the Hong Kong Region*, Hong Kong: Hong Kong University Press, 1983.

Overmyer, Daniel L., *Religions of China: The World as a Living System*, San Francisco: Harper, 1985.

Ross, John, *The Origin of the Chinese People*, Selangor, Malaysia: Pelanduk Publications, 1990. (First published in 1916.)

Selby, Thomas G., *Chinamen at Home*, London: Hodder and Stoughton, 1900.

Smith, Richard J., *China's Cultural Heritage: The Qing Dynasty 1644–1912*, (2nd revised edition), Boulder, Colorado: Westview Press, 1990.

———, *Chinese Almanacs*, Hong Kong: Oxford University Press, 1992.

Stokes, Edward, *Hong Kong's Wild Places: An Environmental Exploration*, Hong Kong: Oxford University Press, 1995.

Thompson, Laurence G., *Chinese Religion: An Introduction*, Belmont, California: Dickenson Publishing Company, Inc., 1969.

Watson, James L., 'Waking the Dragon: Visions of the Chinese Imperial State in Local Myth', in Hugh D. R. Baker and Stephan Feuchtwang (eds.), *An Old State in New Settings: Studies in the Social Anthropology of China in Memory of Maurice Freedman*, Oxford: JASO, 1991, especially at pp. 165–9.

Williams, C. A. S., *Outlines of Chinese Symbolism and Art Motives*, New York: Dover Publications, Inc., 1976. A re-publication of the third revised edition of 1941.

Yang, Yao Lin and Huang, Chong Yue, *Nanyue Kejiawei (Hakka Enclosed Houses in Guangdong and Hong Kong)*, Shenzhen: Wenwu Chuban She, 2001.

Collected Essays on the Culture of the Ancient Yue People in South China, Hong Kong: Urban Council 1993. Pages 64–79 deal with Bronze Age sites in Shenzhen.

Conference Papers on Southeast Asia, The University Museum and Art Gallery: University of Hong Kong, 1995. Pages 383–525 deal with the archaeology of Hong Kong, and pp. 377–382 with 'the preservation and exploitation of cultural relics' in Shenzhen.

Rural Architecture in Hong Kong, Hong Kong: Government Printer for Information Services Department, 1979, and 1989.

The Living Building, Vernacular Environments of South China, Department of Architecture: The Chinese University of Hong Kong, 1995.

The *Journal of the Hong Kong Branch of the Royal Asiatic Society*, published annually since 1961, contains a large number of articles, notes, and queries dealing with the Hong Kong region. It has also published a number of books and symposia brochures. Enquiries to GPO Box 3864, Hong Kong.

The Hong Kong Museum of History, and the Hong Kong Heritage Museum and their predecessors, have issued books and brochures on relevant topics, many of them still in print.

Useful Web Sites

Antiquities and Monuments Office
   http://www.lcsd.gov.hk/CE/Museum/Monument/
Hong Kong Heritage Museum
   http://www.heritagemuseum.gov.hk/
Royal Asiatic Society, Hong Kong Branch
   http://www.royalasiaticsociety.org.hk/
The Hong Kong Museum of History
   http://www.lcsd.gov.hk/CE/Museum/History/

Index

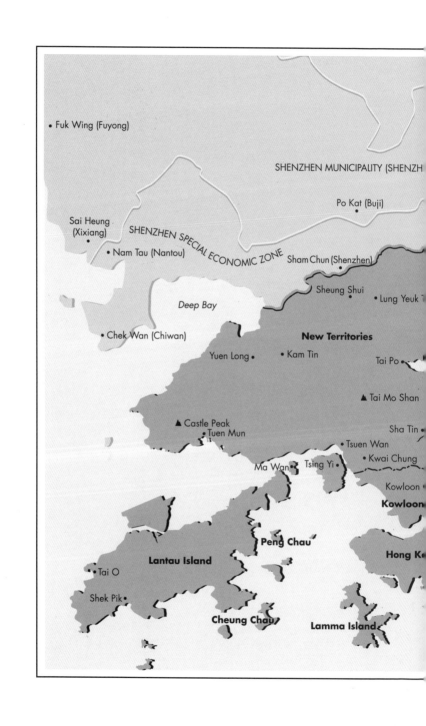

• Fuk Wing (Fuyong)

SHENZHEN MUNICIPALITY (SHENZH

Po Kat (Buji)
•

Sai Heung
(Xixiang)
SHENZHEN SPECIAL ECONOMIC ZONE

• Nam Tau (Nantou)   Sham Chun (Shenzhen)

Sheung Shui
•   • Lung Yeuk

Deep Bay   **New Territories**

• Chek Wan (Chiwan)

Yuen Long •   • Kam Tin   Tai Po •

▲ Tai Mo Shan

▲ Castle Peak   Sha Tin •
• Tuen Mun
• Tsuen Wan

Ma Wan • Tsing Yi • • Kwai Chung

Kowloon •

Kowloon

Peng Chau   **Hong K**

Lantau Island
• Tai O

Shek Pik •

Cheung Chau   **Lamma Island**